MW00328914

A Catechism of Nature

Randy,
With my complements,

Will Brown
Christmastide, 2023

A CATECHISM OF NATURE

Meditations on Creation's Primary Realities

George Willcox Brown III

WIPF & STOCK · Eugene, Oregon

A CATECHISM OF NATURE
Meditations on Creation's Primary Realities

Copyright © 2021 George Willcox Brown III. All rights reserved. Except for brief quotations in critical publications or reviews, no part of this book may be reproduced in any manner without prior written permission from the publisher. Write: Permissions, Wipf and Stock Publishers, 199 W. 8th Ave., Suite 3, Eugene, OR 97401.

Wipf & Stock
An Imprint of Wipf and Stock Publishers
199 W. 8th Ave., Suite 3
Eugene, OR 97401

www.wipfandstock.com

PAPERBACK ISBN: 978-1-7252-9559-9
HARDCOVER ISBN: 978-1-7252-9558-2
EBOOK ISBN: 978-1-7252-9560-5

11/02/21

Naturam expellas furca, tamen usque recurret
et mala perrumpet furtim fastidia victrix.

—HORACE ("LETTER TO ARISTIUS FUSCUS")

CONTENTS

ACKNOWLEDGMENTS

I OWE A DEEP debt of gratitude to the midwives of this volume, the many people who instilled in me, and sustained, my love for wild things and their creator.

First in the order of precedence is my mother, who overflowed with an enthusiasm for natural beauty and growing things. May she rest in peace. Secondly my father, who was my companion and guide on many mountaintops and around many campfires; both of whom saw to it that I was saturated in the story of creation and redemption.

My dear wife, Kate, whose green thumb I envy, and who treats orchids as though they were sentient, has inspired and sustained me in more ways than I could possibly enumerate.

Likewise I am profoundly grateful for the many friends with whom I shared the experiences that were the occasion for this book—the hunting and fishing buddies and the fellow adventurers with whom I have had the privilege of sharing bunks, campfires, blinds, trucks, skiffs, and canoes: CB, CL, MH, BD, JS, RJ, MM, JR, WC and LC, AW and PW, ED and RD, DW, two MWs, three CWs, two CHCs, and more besides. These gentlemen, and several ladies, have made my life rich indeed by sharing with me their love for wild things and adventure, as well as their generosity, skill, encouragement, and friendship. Thank you.

I would also like to give thanks for the late Jim Varnum, a Texan, a naturalist, and a child of Christ, who had forgotten more about prairie ecology than I will ever know, and with whom I shared a special love for trout lilies. Jim was a great naturalist and a great teacher. May he rest in peace.

I also owe a debt of gratitude to a number of institutions that have supported this work in various ways: the Church of the Holy Cross (Dallas), All Saints' Church (Thomasville), the Master Naturalist communities of Texas and Florida, the Texas Parks and Wildlife Foundation, Stewards of the Wild, the Marine Fish Conservation Network, and the Ocean Conservancy.

Special thanks are also due to Dr. Christopher Wells of the Living Church Foundation and to Dr. Ian Markham of Virginia Theological Seminary for providing the conceptual space, leisure, and support that have made this volume a reality. It germinated during a sabbatical fellowship at VTS which they made possible.

I would also like to offer thanks for the many dogs who have been my companions on a number of the adventures that have occasioned these writings. First in my affections is Jeb, with whom I shared nearly every day for over a decade. I feel his absence acutely. Other noteworthy helpers and friends include: Guinness, Rigby, Sien, Little Dude, Bella, Bean, Babe, Holly, Heather, and Gauge, besides dozens of working dogs whose names I have forgotten or never knew, yet without whom many memorable experiences would not have been possible.

And of course I must render most high praise and hearty thanks to the Choreographer of the dance, the Word made flesh, crucified, dead, risen, and ascended, to whom be glory, honor, and dominion, world without end.

GWB

1

INTRODUCTION

THIS VOLUME IS MEANT to address a fundamental problem vexing humanity in our time, the problem of ecological degradation. It also gestures toward the outlines of a solution, drawing on resources from the tradition of Christian ascetical theology.

Following a format suggested by Ephraim Radner in his two volumes introducing natural theology,[1] the present volume pursues its task in two parts: first in a more straightforward, discursive register in this Introduction, and second by means of a series of poetic meditations on various aspects of the natural world. The two parts may be read independently of one another, as may each of the meditations in the second part.

1. The Problem

Life apart from the Creator and out of harmony with creation are phenomena by nature connected to one another. In much the same way that you couldn't know much that's worth knowing about Picasso if you had never seen any of his paintings, so our knowledge of God is to a significant extent a function of our knowledge of what he has made. We will not love what we do not know.

1. Radner, *The World in Shadow*; Radner, *Chasing the Shadow*.

Population growth and urbanization have much to do with this want of knowledge, this disconnection from the primary realities of creation. The population of the world is far larger now than it has ever been. It took almost all of human history, until the year 1804, for the population of the world to reach one billion people. In just over a century, from 1804 to 1927, the population of the world doubled to two billion. The population reached three billion in 1960, four billion in 1974, five billion in 1987, six billion in 1999, and seven billion in 2012. The human population of the planet has not only grown significantly in recent history, but the *rate* of growth has increased as well.

And as the population of the world has grown, the proportion of the population living in cities has increased. Urbanization began in earnest in Europe during the high Middle Ages. In the United States overall, more people lived in the countryside than lived in cities until the 1920s, at which point the balance tipped. It was not until the 1990s that the balance tipped in the American South. According to median estimates, more people now live in the Dallas—Fort Worth metropolitan area (about six and a half million) than lived in all of North America (the United States and Canada) in 1492, when "Columbus sailed the ocean blue."

Nor is this by any means merely an American phenomenon. The population of Lagos, Nigeria, is now about forty-seven times what it was in 1950. There are twenty-one million people living in the greater Lagos metropolitan area. China now has over one hundred cities with populations over one million. Sixteen Chinese cities have populations over ten million (the United States has two: New York and Los Angeles).

Some deny that population growth is a problem. Michael Shellenberger, for example, notes that "technology is a far bigger factor in determining humankind's environmental impacts than fertility rates. Modern agriculture reduces by half the amount of land we need to produce the same amount of food."[2] This however ignores the fact that technologically-driven increases in agricultural efficiency are not evenly distributed, that the places in the

2. Shellenberger, "Bigotry of Environmental Pessimism," para. 17.

world with the largest and fastest increases in population (e.g., Africa and Asia) also tend to be the least agriculturally advanced. Even supposing that agricultural land use efficiency has doubled the world over, the population has increased by a factor of more than seven since 1804, meaning the amount of land converted from wilderness to agriculture would have almost quadrupled in the same period.

Like population growth, the aggregation of people in cities is speeding up, intensifying, and becoming universal, a core feature of a pastiche of phenomena known collectively as globalization. Research indicates that there is a correlation between urbanization and the decline of religious faith, at least in America. Correlation does not entail causation, yet religious faith wanes in our nation as our population has grown and aggregated in cities.

Economic liberalism and its handmaiden, rapid technological advancement, have been important drivers of this demographic shift. The sorts of developments Michael Shellenberger had in mind—genetically modified seeds; the automation of farm equipment, agricultural processes, and animal husbandry; coupled with the radical aggregation of capital and economies of scale—have all made it possible, to grow and harvest food much more efficiently than before (on much less land, with much less human input). There is simply a lot less work for people to do outside of cities, and it takes fewer people to do it.

This has had radical implications not just for the environment, but for the patterns of life that formerly sustained a culture more closely tied to the primary realities of nature. None of it could have come about without the collusion of governments with capital. Roger Scruton maps the contours of that kind of collusion with respect to the rise of "big-box" stores and the concurrent hollowing out of family-owned businesses in small towns:

> Health and safety regulations imposed by the state . . . are responsible for the vast amount of non-biodegradable wrapping that festoons our food; state subsidies and inscrutable bureaucracies are responsible for our system of motorways; and it is the unequal impact of state subsidies

and regulatory burdens that has enabled supermarkets to destroy the local food economy across Europe and America. State-subsidized roads permit supermarkets to operate on the edge of towns and to achieve enormous economies of scale. State imposed planning regulations compel local shopkeepers to build in confined spaces, to maintain costly facades and to serve customers who cannot park outside. State-imposed regulations governing packaging and inspection can be economically obeyed only through centralized processing and distribution, of the kind that supermarkets can manage for themselves. And the economies of scale that supermarkets achieve enable them to preside, from the edge of every town, over the decay of its centre and its destruction as a self-sustaining human habitat. This easy victory for the forces of environmental destruction would be impossible without the unequal burden of state regulations and the unequal benefit of state subsidies, both of which favor the edge-of-town retailer over the local store.[3]

Thanks to free markets and cheap energy, it is now possible to eat tropical fruit year-round in New Hampshire. Thanks to central heat and air-conditioning, I can now be cold in summer and warm in winter. Thanks to hormone therapy and surgical interventions, I can now live my life as a woman if I so choose. Thanks to ready access to safe abortions and other reproductive technologies, my sexuality is now an instrument of my freedom, no longer yoked to biological realities and the responsibilities attendant upon them. Mariners need no longer navigate by the stars.

Patrick Deneen has noted the etymology of the word "culture" and its relationship to nature—as seen in words like "cultivate" or "horticulture"—all being forms of the Latin colere, to "tend" or "till." Culture, to classical thinkers, was the necessary context within which a man could fulfill his potential by being formed in the virtues and by careful attention. Yet for enlightenment figures, like Jean-Jacques Rousseau and Thomas Hobbes, and their intellectual progeny like John Stuart Mill and twentieth century libertarians,

---

3. Scruton, *How to Think Seriously*, 166.

culture in this sense was a negative inhibition on the full flowering of liberty, something to be dispensed with for the sake of the actualization of the individual will.

> This [understanding of culture] was so evident to ancient thinkers that the first several chapters of Plato's *Republic* are devoted not to a discussion of political forms but to the kinds of stories that are appropriate for children. In a suggestive statement winding up his introductory chapter in *The Politics,* Aristotle declares that the first lawmaker is especially praiseworthy for inaugurating governance over "food and sex," that is the two elemental human desires that are most in need of cultivation and civilization: for food, the development of manners that encourage a moderate appetite and civilized consumption, and for sex, the cultivation of customs and habits of courtship, mannered interaction between the sexes, and finally marriage as the "container" of the otherwise combustible and fraught domain of sexuality. People who are "uncultivated" in the consumption of both food and sex, Aristotle obsessed, are the most vicious creatures, literally consuming other humans to slake their base and untutored appetites. Far from being understood as opposites of human nature, customs and manners are understood to be derived from, governed by, and necessary to the realization of human nature.[4]

The very idea of freedom, in some respects the core principle of Western societies, has been revised in such a way as to make it inimical to nature. Freedom is no longer something that must be formed and cultivated in community but is now understood as something basic and atomistic. We have subordinated even the idea of the self to this revised conception of freedom: I am who I choose to be. Or, as theologian Stanley Hauerwas put it, we have become "a people who believe that they should have no story except the story that they choose when they had no story."[5] The primary realities of creation are impediments to the full flowering

4. Deneen, *Why Liberalism Failed*, 68.
5. Hauerwas, "End of American Protestantism," para. 18.

of such autonomy, as may perhaps be most starkly demonstrated in the discourse around "gender identity" in which desire very explicitly trumps nature.

Perhaps this deprecation of the material world and of that aspect of it constituted by the essentially *embodied* life of humans, two sides of the same coin, represents a resurgence of Gnosticism. This theme has been explored by many, notably Wendell Berry in *The Unsettling of America* and elsewhere. The danger posed by this current of thought should be obvious. Carried to its furthest reach, it ends with the destruction of both the material world and the body inhabiting it.

As in any relationship, communion with God must be cultivated, an idea suggested by the fact that the word "cult" also stands in the etymological penumbra of *colere*. Couples that never see or speak with each other naturally drift apart. We must pay attention to what God has said, and nature is his most primordial and exoteric word, what medieval theologians called the *analogia entis*, the analogy of being. The witness of Scripture and Christian tradition is unequivocal on this point. Job says, "Ask the beasts, and they will teach you; the birds of the air, and they will tell you; or the plants of the earth, and they will teach you; and the fish of the sea will declare to you"[6] (Job 12:7–8). And there are the immortal opening words of Psalm 19: "The heavens declare the glory of God; and the firmament showeth his handy-work . . . There is neither speech nor language; but their voices are heard among them. Their sound is gone out into all lands; and their words into the ends of the world." Paul even says that the Gentiles have no excuse for turning away from God: "For what can be known about God is plain to them, because God has shown it to them. Ever since the creation of the world his invisible nature, namely, his eternal power and deity, has been clearly perceived in the things that have been made" (Romans 1:19–20). Augustine writes movingly in Book 10 of his *Confessions* about how creation bears witness to the Creator: "I questioned the earth . . . I questioned the sea and the depths, and

6. The Revised Standard Version will be used throughout unless otherwise noted.

the creeping things which have life . . . I questioned the blowing winds, and the whole air with its inhabitants . . . I questioned the heavens, the sun, moon, stars . . . And they cried out with a loud voice, 'He made us!'"[7]

Likewise, Christian liturgy is rife with reminders of how human nature is situated within the boundaries of the primary realties of the created order. The office of Matins in the Book of Common Prayer begins each day with the recitation of Psalm 95, locating the imperative to worship in humanity's status as creatures bounded within the order of the natural world:

> In his hand are all the corners of the earth; and the strength of the hills is his also. The sea is his, and he made it; and his hands prepared the dry land. O come, let us worship and fall down, and kneel before the Lord our Maker. For he is the Lord our God; and we are the people of his pasture, and the sheep of his hand (Psalm 95: 4–7).

Many ancient liturgical hymns conformed to this pattern too and found themselves incorporated into the Roman Breviary and successor liturgies from various traditions (for example the English translations of Percy Dearmer and others). Hymn 59 (attributed to Gregory the Great) from *The English Hymnal* is typical in recounting some aspects of God's creative energy and resolving into an (implicitly related) exhortation to worship and to ascetical purity:

> Earth's mighty Maker, whose command
> Raised from the sea the solid land,
> And drove each billowy heap away,
> And bade the earth stand firm for aye;
> That so, with flowers of golden hue,
> The seeds of each it might renew;
> And fruit-trees bearing fruit might yield,
> And pleasant pastures of the field;
> Our spirit's rankling wounds efface
> With dewy freshness of thy grace;
> That grief may cleanse each deed of ill,

---

7. Augustine, *Confessions*, 183.

And o'er each lust may triumph still.
Let every soul thy law obey,
And keep from every evil way;
Rejoice each promised good to win,
And flee from every mortal sin.[8]

Less and less in our time and place do we hear the most primordial of God's words—the song, one might say, of creation's fundamental realties. A pastiche of interests colludes to insulate us from nature. Less and less are we able to speak or understand the language of this most primordial word. I was hoping recently to watch the Perseid meteor shower, but when I went into my front yard, the city lights obscured the stars.

2. Philosophical Foundations

In his seminal essay "Politics and Conscience," the Czech dissident (and later president of Czechoslovakia), Václav Havel, opened with an account of his horror upon seeing the smokestacks of a munitions factory billowing smoke as he walked to school as a child: "Each time I saw it," he wrote, "I had an intense sense of something profoundly wrong, of humans soiling the heavens."[9] He went on to consider the reaction of a hypothetical medieval peasant encountering the same spectacle while out hunting: "He would probably think it the work of the Devil and would fall on his knees and pray that he and his kin be saved."

The intuition shared by Havel as a schoolboy and the hypothetical medieval peasant is that the smokestack is not just ugly, but *diabolical*, a moral repugnance. "It seemed to me that, in it, humans are guilty of something, that they destroy something important, arbitrarily disrupting the natural order of things, and that such things cannot go unpunished."[10]

---

8. Dearmer, "Hymn 59," lines 1–16.
9. Havel, "Politics and Conscience," 249.
10. Havel, "Politics and Conscience," 250.

Havel went on to explain that it is the sense of mystery beyond the periphery of the empirical that had been overthrown by a materialist philosophy imposing itself on the social order of Czechoslovakia under communism, all in the name of "science"—that the value of the natural world had been made instrumental, that it was no longer understood to be the home, bordered by the transcendent, within which humanity is embedded. The repugnant smokestacks were, so to speak, an icon of this reality. The result for Czechoslovakia was catastrophic:

> With hedges plowed under and woods cut down, wild birds have died out and, with them, a natural, unpaid protector of the crops against harmful insects. Huge unified fields have led to the inevitable annual loss of millions of cubic yards of topsoil that have taken centuries to accumulate; chemical fertilizers and pesticides have catastrophically poisoned all vegetable products, the earth and the waters . . . It is paradoxical: people in the age of science and technology live in the conviction that they can improve their lives because they are able to grasp and exploit the complexity of nature and the general laws of its functioning. Yet it is precisely these laws which, in the end, tragically catch up with them and get the better of them.[11]

Havel's insight is hardly new. The epigraph of this volume is a quotation from the Roman poet Horace. In a letter to a friend he wrote concerning the superiority of life lived close to nature and within its limits: *Naturam expellas furca, tamen usque recurret et mala perrumpet furtim fastidia victrix.* "You may drive out Nature with a pitchfork, yet she will ever hurry back, and, ere you know it, will burst through your foolish contempt in triumph."[12]

Yet the order of economic and social liberalism into which Havel and his country were liberated from communism is now catching up to its defeated rival in terms of ecological degradation. Writing in the 1920s for the Southern Agrarian manifesto, *I'll Take*

---

11. Havel, "Politics and Conscience," 254.

12. Horace, *Opera*, 219; my translation.

My Stand, fugitive poet John Crowe Ransom decried the "insidious spirit" of industrialism afflicting American life:

> Ambitious men fight, first of all, against nature; they propose to put nature under their heel; this is the dream of scientists burrowing in their cells, and then of the industrial men who beg of their secret knowledge and go out to trouble the earth. But after a certain point this struggle is vain, and we only use ourselves up if we prolong it. Nature wears out man before man can wear out nature; only a city man, a laboratory man, a man cloistered from the normal contact with the soil, will deny that. It seems wiser to be moderate in our expectations of nature, and respectful; and out of so simple a thing as respect for the physical earth and its teeming life comes a primary joy, which is an inexhaustible source of arts and religions and philosophies.[13]

Ransom noted how a farmer may love and identify with his land, how he may perceive nature as a whole through it, by a process of spiritual synecdoche. His engagement with his land can thus become for the farmer the occasion for the awakening in him of a "cosmic consciousness." Yet this is not possible for the industrialist, the banker, or the free marketeer who have taken over American (and increasingly global) agriculture since the nineteenth century. Ransom wrote:

> A man can contemplate and explore, respect and love, an object as substantial as a farm . . . But he cannot contemplate nor explore, respect nor love, a mere turnover, such as an assemblage of "resources," a pile of money, a volume of produce, a market, or a credit system. It is into precisely these intangibles that industrialism would translate the farmer's farm. It means the dehumanization of his life.[14]

13. Ransom, "Reconstructed but Unregenerate," 9.
14. Ransom, "Reconstructed but Unregenerate," 20.

The dehumanization of agriculture is not merely an academic point. Farmers die by suicide at a higher rate than any other occupation in the United States.[15]

Some may find principles about dehumanization disingenuous, extracted from a work such as "I'll Take My Stand," in view of the complicated attitudes toward segregation and related matters espoused by its contributors. Yet leaving aside the imprudence of tout court critiques of Southern Agrarianism on the basis of adjacent moral disputes that were resolved subsequent to its publication, one should note that the principles articulated in "I'll Take My Stand" led its contributors in a variety of directions when it came to America's conflict over segregation and Jim Crow. Whereas Donald Davidson became a strident defender of segregation, Robert Penn Warren became an apologist for integration, very publicly lending his influence to the bourgeoning Civil Rights movement with the publication of "Who Speaks for the Negro?" in 1965.

Be that as it may, it is not just the land and the human life upon it that is degraded by the forces of economic liberalism. We now offload the consequences of our meddling with nature onto the oceans too—on a global scale. Fertilizers from the American heartland run off into the Mississippi River watershed, and thence into the Gulf of Mexico, doing there what they do on land—fertilize—causing massive increases in the growth of phytoplankton and algae, leading to disruptions in food webs and species composition, fish kills and, at the furthest stretch, ecosystem collapse. Similarly, overfishing on an industrial scale is severely depleting fish stocks worldwide. The population of bluefin tuna in the Pacific is estimated to be a mere 4 percent of its preindustrial level (10 percent in the Atlantic). With such severely reduced supply, a single bluefin sold for over three million dollars in Japan in early 2019. Bluefin is one of the most sought-after fish for sushi.

I need hardly mention the plight of rhinoceroses and elephants in Africa, caught between the Scylla of habitat loss and the Charybdis of poaching, the former underwritten by population growth and economic development, and the latter by market

---

15. Weingarten, "Farmers Killing Themselves," para. 18.

demand for ivory and horn. In recent years rhinoceros horn has fetched more than cocaine or gold, ounce per ounce, on the black market in Asia, where it is thought to be an aphrodisiac (despite the fact that it is composed chiefly of keratin, the main ingredient in fingernails).

The list of ecological degradations is seemingly endless and very depressing. And in our time, it is driven primarily by the forces of economic and social liberalism. Yet if these forces are leading to species extinction and potentially irreversible ecological damage—damage that is likely to double back on human development and cause millions to suffer—they cannot plausibly be said to be working. We ought to question the philosophical assumptions underpinning the liberal order and where these have gone wrong. How is it that a medieval peasant would have seen a smokestack soiling the heavens as a satanic incursion into the right order of nature, whereas a modern entrepreneur would likely see the same spectacle and think happily of jobs, profit, and development?

Intuition leads us to the Enlightenment, the gateway through which the Middle Ages became Modernity and peasants became entrepreneurs. And indeed a primary aspect of Enlightenment thought centered precisely on man's relationship to nature. René Descartes, for example, in his *Discourse on Method*, identifies his acquisition of "some general notions respecting physics"[16] that were different in kind from what had until then prevailed in the natural sciences, as the springboard from which humans might "render ourselves the lords and possessors of nature," a position which would redound to "the general good of mankind."

Likewise Francis Bacon, famous for his euphemistic characterization of the scientific method as a form of torture ("putting nature to the test"), in an unfinished work, advocated an epistemological revolution that would result in:

> A restitution and reinvesting . . . of man to the sovereignty and power (for whensoever he shall be able to call the creatures by their true names he shall again command them) which he had in his first state of creation. And to

16. Descartes, *Discourse on Method*, part 6, para. 2.

speak plainly and clearly, it is a discovery of all operations and possibilities of operations from immortality (if
it were possible) to the meanest mechanical practice.[17]

And, as with Descartes's "general good of mankind," Bacon placed
the revolution in the vanguard of which he labored, under the
guiding principle of the "endowment of man's life with new commodities" (i.e., conveniences).

In his exhaustive investigation into the philosophical foundations of the postmedieval world's disenchantment, Charles Taylor identified exactly this instrumentalist turn in Enlightenment
thinking, with respect to humanity's engagement with nature, as a
primary source of modernity's "malaise," and paradoxically one of
the causes of our increasing isolation from nature, and even from
our own life as humans. This indeed stands to reason, if it is true
that human life can be rightly construed only as essentially embedded within nature and subordinated to supernature. Taylor writes,

> In the effort to control our lives, or control nature, we
> have destroyed much that is deep and valuable in them.
> We have been blinded to the importance of equilibria
> which can be upset, but can't be created by instrumental
> rationality. The most important of these in the contem-
> porary debates is obviously the one touching the ecologi-
> cal balance of our entire biosphere.[18]

Notwithstanding the impetus behind the instrumentalist turn—
"the general good of mankind" (Descartes), a more commodious
life (Bacon)—the turn itself has in fact produced not only an ever
more degraded ecosphere, but a world in which Augustine's rest-
lessness has reimposed itself with renewed vigor on human hearts,
a world in which all the maladies that the instrumentalist turn set
out to resolve are felt just as, or more, acutely than ever.

Despite the fact that Bacon and Descartes et al. were theists
(Bacon, for example, explicitly admitted that "all knowledge is to

---

17. Bacon, *Valerius Terminus*, chap. 1, para. 12.
18. Taylor, *A Secular Age*, 317.

be limited by religion"[19]), perhaps the delimiting of the sphere of created nature (which is open to inquiry) from the sphere of divine nature (which is not) serves to suggest a practical severance of the two realms from one another in a way that they are not in fact severed (and were never thought to be in the dominant modes of pre-Enlightenment thought). Perhaps the more ancient understanding of the world as enchanted was correct in some fundamental sense. By ceasing to inquire into the supernatural, to rule it out of the purview of the sciences, no longer acknowledging the permeable barrier between nature and supernature, the contours of human embeddedness within nature, and all of creation's subjugation to its Creator, have been lost and forgotten.

Some of the most perceptive thinkers of the recent past have maintained an intuition of creation's permeability, its enchantment, and therefore of its non-instrumental value, while at the same time having lost sight of its reference to a supernatural order within which it is embedded or sublimated as in a hierarchy of being. The noted essayist and environmentalist Edward Abbey was one such thinker. His 1968 book *Desert Solitaire* is an extended reflection on the enchantment of the area in and around the Arches National Monument in eastern Utah, the first in a long series of Abbey's justly celebrated non-fiction environmental writings. Abbey was a strident defender of the natural world's non-instrumental value, yet he cursorily rejected a transcendent source for that value. "What is the difference between the Lone Ranger and God?" he once quipped, "There really is a Lone Ranger."[20]

The poet Robinson Jeffers, whom Abbey greatly admired, was another such thinker, and a more subtle one. Jeffers's poetry rises to the level of prophecy in its penetrating critique of the ecological and psychic corrosiveness of the Enlightenment turn of thought sketched above, in its subordination of the totality of nature to an atomistic conception of human freedom. In "Shine, Republic," for example, Jeffers notes the incompatibility of the implicit voluntarism of Hobbes and Rousseau with the Baconian/

19. Bacon, *Valerius Terminus*, chap. 1, para. 4.
20. Abbey, *A Voice Crying*, 10.

Cartesian instrumentalist view of nature embodied in the American republic:

> And you, America, that passion made you. You were not
> born to prosperity,
>   you were born to love freedom.
> You did not say "en masse," you said "independence." But
> we cannot have
>   all the luxuries and freedom also.
> Freedom is poor and laborious; that torch is not safe but
> hungry, and often
>   requires blood for its fuel.
> You will tame it against it burn too clearly, you will hood
> it like a kept
>   hawk, you will perch it on the wrist of Caesar.
> But keep the tradition, conserve the forms, the obser-
> vances, keep the spot
>   sore. Be great, carve deep your heel-marks.
> The states of the next age will no doubt remember you,
> and edge their love
>   of freedom with contempt of luxury.[21]

Albert Gelpi, in his introduction to Jeffers's poetry, notes how Jeffers's "inhumanism" and pantheism, which Gelpi identifies as a form of Calvinist agnosticism, makes natural history into a "divine tragedy." Gelpi writes:

> Even near the end, in "Carmel Point," [Jeffers] is still only
> able to say: "We must uncenter our minds from ourselves:
> / We must unhumanize our views a little." The telltale
> verb is "must"; not here or ever: "I *have* uncentered my
> mind from myself." Consciousness is indistinguishable
> from self, and vice versa. Language is the instrument
> and embodiment of consciousness; poetry is the voice of
> the human and can never be the voice of nature. Jeffers
> expresses in words the desire to "become confident / As
> the rock and ocean that we are made from." But we are
> not made from rock or ocean, and confidence or lack of

---

21. Jeffers, *Wild God*, 154.

confidence is a human experience, projected here onto rock and wave out of human need.[22]

One can see this most acutely in Jeffers's descriptions of death, surely nature's permeable boundary *par excellence.* In "Cawdor" Jeffers describes death in exclusively materialist terms:

> Pain and pleasure
> are not to be thought
> Important enough to require balancing: these flashes of
> post-mortal felicity
> by mindless decay
> Played on the breaking harp by no means countervailed
> the excess of
> previous pain. Such discords
> In the passionate terms of human experience are not
> resolved, nor worth it.
> The
> ecstasy in its timelessness
> Resembled the eternal heaven of the Christian myth, but
> actually the
> nerve-pulp as organ of pleasure
> Was played to pieces in a few hours, before the day's end.
> Afterwards it
> entered importance again
> Through worms and flesh-dissolving bacteria. The per-
> sonal show was over,
> the mountain earnest continued
> In the earth and air.[23]

What remains, after the exclusion of the supernatural from the worldview of one as much inclined to mysticism as Jeffers, is the exclusively natural: "the mountain earnest," or trees, rocks, fog, ocean, and darkness. But it is in such things that Jeffers finds the totality of the story of being. "But here is the final unridiculous peace," he proclaims in "Hooded Night," "Here is reality."[24]

22. Jeffers, *Wild God,* 14.
23. Jeffers, *Wild God,* 88.
24. Jeffers, *Wild God,* 148.

Yet the way out of the malaise and ecological degradation wrought by the liberal order's instrumentalist engagement with nature surely lies in another direction, a direction that does not lead to a materialistic "divine tragedy," with fog and darkness at the farthest reach of human aspiration. In the meditations of the second part of this volume, I mean to gesture in just such an alternative direction. These meditations are outgrowths of my experience of what might be called, in a Neoplatonic register, natural contemplation. They suggest the possibility of a recovery of the supernatural, a scrutiny of the permeable boundaries of the natural world, and thus they suggest that a solution to the problems facing contemporaneity rests in *metanoia*, a penitential reorientation of perspective. I hope therefore to avoid the rejoinder, often leveled against critics of the Enlightenment, that appeals to the "commodities" (Bacon) afforded us by the revolution in the natural sciences—penicillin, air-conditioning and so forth. It is perfectly possible to admit the goodness of such things while suggesting the epistemological underpinnings of their discovery to have been defective. In any event, the fact that such discoveries and inventions were made in *this* way does not foreclose the possibility that they—or better ones—might have been made in some other way.

The Neoplatonic character of these essays is perhaps best captured by the tradition issuing from Pseudo-Dionysius the Areopagite, who characterized natural contemplation precisely as a direction, a "path," as I too have suggested. Dionysius said:

> We cannot know God in his nature, since this is unknowable and is beyond the reach of mind or of reason. But we know him from the arrangement of everything, because everything is, in a sense, projected out from him, and this order possesses certain images and semblances of his divine paradigms.[25]

This is a strand of thought central to the many Fathers of the early Church, riffing in one way or another on a theme running through Scripture (e.g., Romans 1:19–21). As I have noted above, God may

---

25. Pseudo-Dionysius, *Divine Names*, 869C–869D.

be known through the contemplation of created things, imbued as they are by their creator (the *Logos*) with intelligible traces (*logoi*)—their harmonious order, the manifest wisdom of their creation and so forth—of himself.

Following this line of thought from Dionysius, Maximus the Confessor fixes natural contemplation in a robust theology of creation *ex nihilo*:

> God himself bring[s] into existence out of nothing the very being of all created things, since He is beyond being and even infinitely transcends the attribution of beyond-beingness. For . . . it is He who has given to nature the energy which produces its forms, and who has established the very is-ness of beings by virtue of which they exist.[26]

Thus humanity, existing as we do in the hierarchy of being somewhere between the beasts and the angels, the natural and the supernatural, with a foot (as it were) in both worlds, precisely *is*, in some sense, the permeable boundary between nature and supernature. This insight shows up Jeffers's conception of death (the limit of human life and, therefore, of the natural world) in such a tragic light.

It is our (humanity's) standing simultaneously on the highest rung of the ladder of nature and the lowest rung of supernature that underwrites our status as priests of creation. Michael Harrington traces this line of thought in the *Liber Ambiguorum* of Maximus, noting that, for Maximus, as for many Christians in the Neoplatonic tradition, the one who contemplates in a certain sense becomes the object of his contemplation. Humans are thus "responsible for weaving together the intelligible and the sensible into a form of reality distinct from both by themselves."[27] Such contemplative engagement with the natural world "imbues the world with the form of God, and so establishes the world on a new level. It is a creative theophany."

---

26. Palmer et al., *The Philokalia*, 2:165.
27. Harrington, "Creation and Natural Contemplation," 191–193.

Natural contemplation, of the kind that the essays in the second part of this volume are meant to reveal, is thus not merely for the edification of the contemplative, the "nature lover." It is rather the very activity by which the world's salvation might be achieved, precisely by establishing the world on a new (and higher) level, by imbuing it with the form of God. For, as Dionysius suggests,

> Salvation is that which preserves things in their proper places without change, conflict, or collapse toward evil, that it keeps them all in peaceful and untroubled obedience to their proper laws . . . this Salvation, benevolently operating for the preservation of the world, redeems everything in accordance with the capacity of things to be saved.[28]

That is to say, salvation is a form of *conservation*, the preservation of things in the form that God intends. And they are preserved (or, perhaps, rescued) by means of a form of contemplative engagement, an engagement on account of which created realities are internalized by humans, incorporated into human subjectivity, and prayerfully submitted to God by obedience. But the prerequisite for this form of engagement is an attunement to natural realities as they are—i.e., and not instrumentally—and a recognition of the continuity of nature and supernature, a continuity located precisely in human life, all under the rubric of God's sovereignty and transcendence, and the acknowledgement of his having created the world in wisdom and benevolence.

Any other way, according to Maximus, runs the risk of "attributing to human ingenuity more power to establish a perfect order of things than to God, and to an ingenious mutilation of nature the ability to make good shortcomings in God's creation."[29] And yet this "attributing to human ingenuity more power to establish a perfect order" is precisely the turn of Western culture following Bacon, Descartes, et al., now flowering in a rich profusion in the various patterns of thought emanating from Silicon Valley and elsewhere.

28. Pseudo-Dionysius, *Divine Names*, 869D–897A.
29. Palmer et al., *The Philokalia*, 2:270–271.

But Christianity has always insisted on a robust doctrine of creation, of God's having ordered the world in wisdom and benevolence. Scripture opens with just such an insistence. God made the world, declared it to be good, and set humanity in the midst of it to "till it and keep it" (Genesis 2:15), and God has never relinquished his claim to it. As I have noted, the daily round of Christian liturgical prayer has, for many centuries, begun in the same way, as with the office of Matins opening with Psalm 95, the *Venite*,—"the sea is his and he made it, and his hands prepared the dry land," etc. Joseph Ratzinger (later Pope Benedict XVI) noted a thread of continuity running between the creation myths of various cultures concerning the orientation of all things towards God's transcendence.

> The danger that confronts us today in our technological civilization is that we have cut ourselves off from this primordial knowledge, which serves as a guidepost and which links the great cultures, and that an increasing scientific know-how is preventing us from being aware of the fact of creation.[30]

Ratzinger went on to note how Scripture attributes the devastation of Israel in the Babylonian captivity to exactly this kind of ecological sin:

> Even after the exile people continued to ask themselves: Why did God do this to us? Why this excessive punishment, which God seems to be punishing himself with? (They could have had no idea at the time of how he would take all punishment on himself on the cross and of how he would let himself be wounded in the course of his love-history with humankind.) How could that be? In the Second Book of Chronicles the answer reads: All the many sins that the prophets inveighed against could not, in the end, be sufficient reason for such inordinate punishment. The reason had to lie somewhere deeper, somewhere closer to the heart of things. The Second Book of Chronicles describes this deepest cause in the

---

30. Ratzinger, *In the Beginning*, 28.

following words: "The land enjoyed its sabbaths. All the days that it lay desolate it kept sabbath, to fulfill seventy years" (2 Chronicles 36:21).

What this means is that the people had rejected God's rest, its leisure, its worship, its peace, and its freedom, and so they fell into the slavery of activity. They brought the earth into the slavery of their activity and thereby enslaved themselves. Therefore God had to give them the sabbath that they denied themselves. In their "no" to the God-given rhythm of freedom and leisure they departed from their likeness to God and so did damage to the earth. Therefore they had to be snatched from their obstinate attachment to their own work. God had to begin afresh to make them his very own, and he had to free them from the domination of activity. *Operi Dei nihil praeponatur* ["let nothing be preferred to the work of God"]: The worship of God, his freedom, and his rest come first. Thus and only thus can the human beings truly live.[31]

3. Theological Foundations

Come now, I will tell thee—and do thou hearken to my saying and carry it away—the only two ways of search that can be thought of. The first, namely, that *It is*, and that it is impossible for it not to be, is the way of belief, for truth is its companion. The other, namely, that *It is not*, and that it must needs not be—that, I tell thee, is a path that none can learn of at all. For thou canst not know what is not—that is impossible—nor utter it . . . . for it is the same thing that can be thought and that can be.[32]

—Parmenides of Elea

In his book, *How to Change Your Mind: What the New Science of Psychedelics Teaches Us About Consciousness, Dying, Addiction, Depression, and Transcendence*, Michael Pollan quotes a scientist

31. Ratzinger, *In the Beginning*, 31–32.
32. Parmenides, "The Real," 79–80.

who participated in a study of psychedelic drugs at Johns Hopkins in 1999. The experience changed his life.

> Turner is now an ordained Zen monk, yet he is also still a physicist, working for a company that makes helium neon lasers. I asked him if he felt any tension between his science and his spiritual practice. "I don't feel there's a contradiction. Yet what happened at Hopkins has influenced my physics. I realize there are just some domains that science will not penetrate. Science can bring you to the big bang, but it can't take you beyond it. You need a different kind of apparatus to peer into that.[33]

The book of Genesis makes a similar point: an impenetrable veil lies at the bedrock of creation, and the domain God inhabits lies beyond that veil—or perhaps just that "God" is our name for that unutterable Being beyond being. "In the beginning God"—The very heart of the orthodox Christian consensus remarkably claims that this is all we can know by means of positive knowledge, even when aided by divine revelation: In the beginning, God.

Yet sense experience, empirical science and deduction, cannot take us even that far. The natural sciences are, by definition, concerned with nature, and the doctrine of creation is the doctrine of the creation of created nature. The question of what is anterior to created nature thus rules itself out of bounds when it comes to the discourse of the natural sciences. This is not a peripheral insight with respect to Christianity, but rather sits at the very center. In the eighth century, St. John of Damascus, Doctor of the Church, in his *Exact Exposition of the Orthodox Faith* wrote:

> In the case of God, however, it is impossible to explain what He is in His essence, and it befits us the rather to hold discourse about His absolute separation from all things. For He does not belong to the class of existing things: not that He has no existence, but that He is above all existing things, nay even above existence itself. For if all forms of knowledge have to do with what exists, assuredly that which is above knowledge must certainly be

33. Pollan, *Change Your Mind*, 73.

also above essence: and, conversely, that which is above essence will also be above knowledge.[34]

It is curious to think that intellectual technology has made so little fundamental progress, not just since the time of John of Damascus, but since the Eleatic philosophers of the sixth century BC. We must begin therefore in the company of Parmenides: "thou canst not know what is not – that is impossible – nor utter it.[35]" That What Is Not should utter itself, though, and that such an Utterance should be wrapped up intrinsically with the discourse of What Is, *can* be known, only not by an empirical way.

We must begin then with the "data" of being, the data of created nature. We must begin with the acknowledgement of nature's "givenness." I mean this in the philosophical sense of its being a fact of the matter: "The world," said Wittgenstein in the *Tractatus Logico-Philosophicus*, "is all that is the case."[36]

I also mean "the data of nature" in the related theological sense of nature's being a "gift" that is given to us. Both senses of nature's "givenness" are facets of what I mean by the "data" of nature—the word "data" being a participle of the Latin *dare*, "to give."

Next we may contend with the question of who gave this gift, and to whom? And of course, as Christians, we must attend to the witness of Scripture, the dual creation narratives from Genesis 1 and 2 being our lodestars on this score. "In the beginning, God created the heavens and the earth" (Genesis 1:1); "The LORD God took the man and put him in the garden of Eden to till it and keep it" (Genesis 2:15). Thus, while there may be other recipients of the gift of nature, it is at least given to man, who is also enmeshed within it, both to cultivate it and to care for it—which is what "tilling" and "keeping" connote respectively. "Tilling" means a concern for nature's flourishing, and "keeping" means that we are to be invested in this undertaking as stewards and heirs, not slavishly as bondsmen, let alone as rapacious usurpers.

---

34. John of Damascus, *Orthodox Faith*, 4.

35. Parmenides, "The Real," 79.

36. Wittgenstein, *Tractatus*, 5.

Here arises a vexing question: why? Why did God create the heavens and the earth, human beings, and all the rest? In the Christian account, at least, it costs him an awful lot of grief, and would it not have been better for him to have saved himself the trouble? A myriad of answers might be given—indeed they *have* been given—to this question. But at the most fundamental level, we can say that God created the world, because he wanted it to be created, he desired that it should be. He affirmed it in its being, said Yes to it, assented to it. And it is precisely this divine "Yes" that brings the world to be in the same gesture. God makes the world because he wants it made. The Being beyond being desired that being should be.

We may infer from this fact alone that being—created nature—is good, and Genesis says so explicitly, in case there were any doubt:

> And God saw everything that he had made, and behold, it was very good. And there was evening and there was morning, a sixth day. Thus the heavens and the earth were finished, and all the host of them. And on the seventh day God finished his work which he had done, and he rested on the seventh day from all his work which he had done (Genesis 1:31—2:2).

Completing the circle then, God has made this world because he wanted it made, because in some sense he delights in it. He has set us in the midst of it, as a part of it, and has given it to us, to cultivate it and to care for it. This cultivation and care are thus duties and obligations for which we are answerable to God, to whom the world always belongs, because God has never relinquished his claim to what he made. Actions, habits, ways of thinking (ideologies), and ways of life that are incompatible with this mission are therefore wrong. They are derelictions of the highest kind of duty, the kind that we owe to God. Such derelictions are thus, one may say, serious sins. This, for Christians, must be the foundation for environmental ethics.

2

ON LANGUAGE AND TRANSCENDENCE

1.

ACCORDING TO PETER MATTHIESSEN (channeling the great Africanist G.W.B. Huntingford), the San people of southern Africa speak of a former time when "wild animals spoke with men, and all were friends.[1]"

Through the millennia of Bantu expansion, the San have been dispossessed by their neighbors' need for arable land and pasture for their animals. The San, being hunter-gatherers, can live almost anywhere and so have landed in arid corners of the Kalahari and such places no one else wants. Whig history has taken a dim view of the San predilection for communion with creation's primary realties, and they continue to be pressed by various government-mandated modernization schemes. In recent years San hunters found themselves hauled into court for violations of Botswana's ham-fisted and counterproductive all-out ban on hunting instituted in 2012—i.e., for doing what they have done for more than forty thousand years. Genetic studies have shown that the San carry among the oldest Y chromosome haplogroups to have diverged from the main trunk of humanity's genetic family tree.

---

1. Matthiessen, *The Tree*, 59.

Herein lies an intimation of prelapsarian innocence, of a time when the self as world-limit evinced a porousness now lost, when the sound of the Lord God could be heard in the garden in the cool of the day. I once heard Allan Savory say that whoever you are, when you come to Africa, you are coming home, because mankind was born there. I have known others to express feeling this strongly when they first visited the Holy Land, where man was reborn from above in the City of David, the very crossroads where the human family had come up from the south and turned from itself to go east and north, to fill the earth and subdue it.

2.

When I was an undergraduate, studying Wittgenstein's *Tractatus*, I became enamored with "Russell's paradox," a presumed problem in the foundations of mathematics and naïve set theory, around which much work was being done in Bertrand Russell's day, by Russell himself, and by such luminaries as Gottlob Frege and Georg Cantor. Russell's paradox, in brief, notes that in order for the "set of all sets not members of themselves" to be a member of itself, it has to *not* be a member of itself. If it is, then it isn't. And if it isn't, then it is.

Dimly following the contours of Wittgenstein's argument, I intuited that there was an analogy to the paradox in spiritual experience and that the resolution of this analogous, spiritual paradox was one way of construing the work of God in the person of Christ. The spiritual problem was eloquently and famously expressed by Augustine in the opening passages of his *Confessions*, where he asks God: "How can I call unto you when you are already in me? Or from whence would you come unto me? Or where beyond heaven and earth could I go that from thence my God could come unto me, when he has said 'I fill heaven and earth'?"[2]

To begin with—and this is where Wittgenstein's early work is useful—there is a strong connection between systems of

2. Augustine, *Confessions*, 4; Augustine, *Confessiones*, Book 1, Chap. 2, lines 4–5; my translation.

mathematics on the one hand and human language ("How can I call unto you?") on the other. And insofar as spiritual experience operates most fundamentally on a plane transcending language, the very possibility of such fundamental spiritual experience entails a resolution of the problem. Over the course of his career, Wittgenstein himself seems also to have intuited this connection. In his *Remarks on the Foundations of Mathematics*, he refers to philosophical problems as a "sickness" and suggests that the remedy is only possible through "a changed mode of thought and life"—perhaps what Christians call "metanoia," "repentance." In an even more remarkable passage from his diaries (later translated and published under the title *Culture and Value*), Wittgenstein writes:

> I read: 'No man can say that Jesus is the Lord, but by the Holy Ghost.'—And it is true: I cannot call him *Lord*; because that says nothing to me. I could call him 'the paragon', 'God' even – or rather, I can understand it when he is called thus; but I cannot utter the word 'Lord' with meaning. *Because I do not believe* that he will come to judge me; because *that* says nothing to me. And it could say something to me, only if I lived *completely* differently.[3]

3.

By way of reformulating the problem, one might ask: how can a man know himself when his self subsists at the very limit of his world and his experience, like the eye's relation to the visual field? In order to know ourselves as we are, it is necessary that we should get behind or outside of ourselves. Just so, to know the transcendent God, we must learn to look upward, toward what is beyond the limit—the limit constituted by our very selves—beyond the limit of this world, beyond the limit within which thought, language, and sense perception all operate. In the opening verses of "Ash Wednesday," T.S. Eliot circled around the problem:

3. Wittgenstein, *Culture and Value*, 33.

If the lost word is lost, if the spent word is spent
If the unheard, unspoken
Word is unspoken, unheard;
Still is the unspoken word, the Word unheard,
The Word without a word, the Word within
the world and for the world;
And the light shone in darkness and
Against the Word the unstilled world still whirled
About the centre of the silent Word.[4]

William James likewise perceived something of the problem, or swam in it, or addressed it obliquely in *The Varieties of Religious Experience*. Simply to raise the question of "varieties" of religious experience is to raise the question of heterogeneous domains of discourse. One is cutting below the level of languages, so distinctive in their variety. Thus at their core, where their commonality lies, there is the experience, by definition, of the ineffable, the experience of what is somehow below (or above or beyond) the variegation of language, beyond the "region of dissimilitude."[5]

In the eleventh century, Hugh of Saint Victor encouraged monks to give up intellectual discourse, because it is the job of monks to *weep* and not to teach.[6] It is perhaps no coincidence that his advice coincided with the beginning of the process of European urbanization, a process we now see reaching a crescendo on a global scale in our own day. It wasn't until the 1990s that the American South saw more people living in cities than in the countryside. Indeed it seems harder to *love* in cities, where we spend our time ever more radically self-limited, staring at our phones, even our transient relationships with checkout clerks increasingly mediated by screens and keypads. It gets harder and harder for us to break through our self-limits, our limits as selves, and to commune with what is above and beyond (*in illa quae ultra sunt*), and

4. Eliot, "Ash Wednesday," part 5, 1–9.

5. Augustine, *Confessions*, 123; Augustine, *Confessiones*, Book 7, Chap. 10, line 6; my translation.

6. Hugh of St. Victor, *Didascalicon*, 114.

thus to engage in a more integrated way with what is within and below. It has perhaps been impossible for a long time.

In *Concluding Unscientific Postscript to Philosophical Fragments*, Kierkegaard responded sharply to Gotthold Lessing's complaint about being unable to leap across the "ugly, broad ditch" separating time and eternity. Kierkegaard said, "Leaping means to belong essentially to the earth and to respect the law of gravity so that the leap is merely the momentary, but flying means to be set free from telluric conditions, something that is reserved exclusively for winged creatures."[7]

4.

When I was in Africa a few years ago, the shepherd trees were flowering, filling the air with their trademark, slightly acrid sweetness. Like those of mankind, the shepherd tree's roots go deep into the African soil. In 1974 a specimen was found in the central Kalahari with a root depth of sixty-eight meters. The San people know how to get water from old hollow trunks, water brought up from the depths by the tree's roots. I saw among the trees a herd of rhinoceroses whose horns had been removed by the stewards of that particular land after six had been lost to poachers over the course of a few short years—a bleak manifestation of how ignorance can collude with "free" markets to create an ecological crisis on the other side of the world. The rhinos looked ridiculous, but they were alive.

I thought how that landscape is an icon of our predicament. The insularity of humanity, the impermeable boundaries of our selfhoods, of our discourses and desires, it is all a great conspiracy of alienation—from the land, from the plant and animal kingdoms over which we have been set as stewards, from one another, and from our own selves. We have lost the ability to speak and understand the language of creation. It is lost in our flight from one another, in the radical heterogeneity of our crazy little identities

---

7. Kierkegaard, *Concluding Unscientific Postscript*, 124.

and discourses. In *Laudato Si'* Pope Francis wrote precisely in such terms: "We have to realize that a true ecological approach always becomes a social approach; it must integrate questions of justice in debates on the environment, so as *to hear both the cry of the earth and the cry of the poor.*"[8]

On my flight home from Africa, as we began our final approach, I looked out on a land divided and conquered by agriculture, giving way to the vast murdered prairie of northeast Texas. I thought of W.H. Auden:

> Nothing can save us that is possible:
> We who must die demand a miracle.[9]

I was returning to my church's feast of title, Holy Cross Day, the commemoration of that "most impossible possible,"[10] the flowering of life from the tree of death, set up at the *axis mundi*, the great crossroads of the human family. I thought of its root structure cracking the hard mantle of human pride, creating an oasis of living water in the midst of all this aridity. I thought of how urgent it is for us to learn again to weep and to speak—and to hear again the alien voices of our own fragmented humanity, to hear and to conduct the earth's own weeping, murmuring, and singing.

Through the polycarbonate resin of the plane's window, I silently exhorted the silent land below me: *Benedicite omnia opera Domini, Domino.* "O all ye works of the Lord, bless ye the Lord"[11] (Daniel 3:57).

---

8. Francis, *Laudato Si,'* 38.

9. Auden, "For the Time Being," 146–147.

10. Derrida, *On the Name*, 43.

11. *The Vulgate Bible*

3

REASON AND THE DESTINY
OF ANIMAL LIFE

So out of the ground the LORD God formed every beast
of the field and every bird of the air, and brought them
to the man to see what he would call them; and whatever
the man called every living creature, that was its name.
(Genesis 2:19)

ONE OF THE JOYS of spending time in the wilderness is the acquaintance one makes over time with fellow creatures in the animal kingdom. I have spent many happy days observing wildlife, from shorebirds and waterfowl in south Texas, to baboons and predators and ungulates in the African veld, to flying fish and eclectus parrots in the South Pacific. This observation has been the occasion for some thought on the nature of animality against the backdrop of Christian faith.

Among the truths that obtrude most forcefully on the consciousness of the observer of wildlife is the gulf that separates the observer from the observed, our kinship on the scale of being, under another aspect, notwithstanding. There is an arresting and graphic passage in Matthiessen's *The Tree Where Man was Born* (1972) about a pack of wild dogs killing and eating a zebra foal on the plains of east Africa. The most remarkable and counterintuitive facet of the scene is the impassivity of the foal's mother. It's a conspicuous warning to mind the metaphysical gap, upsetting our easy proclivity for anthropomorphism:

> Once more the mare rushed at the dogs, and once again, but already she seemed resigned to what was happening, and did not follow up her own attacks. . . . Between her legs, her foal was being eaten alive, and mercifully, she did nothing . . . . Unmarked, the mare turned and walked away. . . . Flanks pressed together, ears alert, her band awaited her; nearby, other zebra clans were grazing. Soon the foal's family, carrying the mare with it, moved away, snatching at the grass as they ambled westward.[1]

I witnessed a similar scene with lions and impala in the lowveld far to the south of the Serengeti Plains. Animals do have a kind of dignity of their own. But it is their own, further down the scale of being from us and over the horizon of rationality. While it is not the same as ours, it seems necessary to say that the dignity of animals is no less *real* for its differences. Goodness is all of a kind and flows from a common source. *Bonum est diffusivum sui.*

St. Ambrose of Milan noted that "there are three things which united together conduce to the salvation of man: the Sacrament, the Wilderness, Fasting[2]" (*Catena Aurea* on Luke 4). The first and the last of these three conduits of salvation come naturally into sharper relief during Lent. But the Wilderness is seldom considered other than as an abstraction connoting the sort of quiet and solitude one may find in one's own room with the door shut (Matthew 6:6).

Jesus and his first disciples appear to have taken the wilderness more literally, spending time in wild places to cultivate communion with the Creator, not least, one may surmise, by beholding his works unmediated. One thinks of the forty days in the wilderness at the beginning of Jesus' public ministry, how the gospels show him regularly seeking out lonely places (Luke 4:42), or how Paul withdrew for a time into the vastness of Arabia after his conversion (Galatians 1:17). One thinks too of the withdrawal of Christians

1. Matthiessen, *The Tree*, 119.
2. Aquinas, *Catena Aurea*, 144.

into the wildernesses of upper Egypt and Cappadocia during the fourth century at the foundation of Christian monasticism.

Every dog owner will know that animals have an emotional life. But their emotions, like their dignity, are their own; they are not man's. In *That Hideous Strength* (1945), C.S. Lewis described a tame bear's experience of what, in ourselves, we call appetitive desire.

> The appetencies which a human mind might disdain as cupboard loves were for him quivering and ecstatic aspirations which absorbed his whole being, infinite yearnings, stabbed with the threat of tragedy and shot through with the colours of Paradise.[3]

I recall taking my dog, Jeb, for his afternoon walk. I ordered him to heel, as he had trotted too far in front, and we were approaching an intersection. I normally give that command when I am standing still and wait for him to come to heel before moving on. But that time I said it as I continued walking, and Jeb looked at me as though I had two heads. By that time Jeb and I had gotten to know one another pretty well through years of cohabitation, and I recognized his confusion and therefore stopped and told him again to heel. He obediently pranced over and took his wonted place on my left. As we walked on, I amused myself pointlessly explaining the situation to him:

> I know my movement confused you, but you can heel even when we're both moving. Movement is one of the excellences we share. In a way, you're even better at it than I am. Which brings me to another point. It's not that you lack excellence altogether, it's just that my excellences are of a more excellent kind than yours. But some of yours, considered in themselves, even excel mine. You're much faster than me, for example.

Jeb glanced up at me. By now he can tell by the tone of my voice when I am in a philosophical mood, and he knows to ignore it

---

3. Lewis, *That Hideous Strength*, 303.

until I say the word "okay," and he is at liberty to pursue his main interests: wrestling, careering about, and squirrels.

Man is the only animal in a position to understand and care about the pasts and futures of things—including himself, other animals, and nature at the larger scale—or to recognize that existences have an orientation, what Aristotle called a *telos* or "final cause."[4] I once saw an entire hillside cleared of marula trees by a herd of elephants. The elephants would push over a tree, eat a few leaves from the upper branches, then push over another tree and repeat the process. Since a single elephant can eat upwards of six hundred pounds of vegetation every day, it's easy to see the problem—the incompatibility of such behavior with the ends of various existences, including, ultimately, those of the elephants themselves. It's also easy to see why a Tanzanian cassava farmer might feel differently about elephants than a Dupont Circle liberal.

Just so, it is a matter of complete indifference to a tarpon how his presence or absence might impact the ecosphere or economy of the Gulf Coast of the United States. Like the elephant, he simply goes where there's an abundance of the sorts of things he likes to eat. No more food, no more tarpon. And in this respect, he is no different from his food. The tarpon eats the mullet, the mullet eats the shrimp, the shrimp eats the plankton, and if an industrial plant has killed off the plankton from the seawater of a particular area, the effects ripple through the food web and thence back into the human economy.

In the early 1990s the cod fishery along Canada's Atlantic coast disappeared almost overnight due to overfishing. The ecosystem was pushed beyond what it could bear, and the fishery simply and suddenly collapsed. There were practically no fish left. In 1992 the fishery was closed for good, and the cod population has yet to recover almost thirty years later. Neither the cod, nor their prey, nor the ocean itself care a whit about the collapse. But tens of thousands of people in hundreds of coastal communities suddenly found themselves unemployed, and a way of life centuries in the making came to an end.

4. Aristotle, *Parts of Animals*, 36.

God said to Noah and his sons, "The fear of you and the dread of you shall be upon every beast of the earth, and upon every bird of the air, upon everything that creeps on the ground and all the fish of the sea; into your hand they are delivered. Every moving thing that lives shall be food for you; and as I gave you the green plants, I give you everything" (Genesis 9:1–3).

With great power comes great responsibility. Our reason enables us to approach the boundaries of its own capacity and gesture beyond it, toward eternity. Here lies the mystery of our status as priests and kings of creation. Reason, the thing that separates us from brute beasts, does not liberate us *from* animality, but it liberates animality itself, for the actualization of a potential that cannot be actualized without reason. Cod do not fall into a depression when they run up against the limits of their codness; they accept it without wonder. And people who see our own species as the chief obstacle to conservation are only half right. Man is at once the chief obstacle and the only possible solution.

4

EDGE EFFECT

THE GOSPELS INDICATE THAT mankind lives on a cosmic boundary between the treading down of Jerusalem and the end of all things. The Lord called this borderland "the times of the Gentiles" (Luke 21:24). Havel states: "We must honor with the humility of the wise the limits of that natural world and the mystery which lies beyond them, admitting that there is something in the order of being which evidently exceeds all our competence."[1]

Cardinal Newman too wrote about this metaphysical boundary, of how the course of human history veered sharply at the incarnation when the Maker of all things crept quietly across the border of space-time:

> For so it was, that up to Christ's coming in the flesh, the course of things ran straight towards this end, nearing it by every step; but now, under the Gospel, that course has . . . altered its direction, as regards His second coming, and runs, not towards the end, but along it, and on the brink of it; and is at all times equally near that great event, which, did it run towards, it would at once run into.[2]

---

1. Havel, *Open Letters*, 267.
2. Newman, *Sermons*, 1336.

Ecologists speak of an "edge effect," of the biotic conditions marked by the boundaries between habitats. Where woodland runs up against cultivated land, for example, hunters know to look for cottontails or bobwhite quail. Sunlight and wind create the right conditions for the kinds of plant growth such animals like, shade-averse shrubs and vines, leafy forbs, and so forth.

There is a temporal edge effect too—dusk and dawn, sharpening the attention of the wading bird and fisherman alike, temperature differentials and changes in light and barometric pressure stirring the frogs and the fish to action.

The borders between changing seasons awaken the migratory instincts of many species. It takes four generations of monarch butterfly to make their annual pilgrimage from the Sierra Madre mountains of Mexico to their summer habitat in southern Canada and back again to Mexico. Some unfathomable instinct urges the generations there and back, wave on wave across a continent of mortality and reproduction.

Over the Memorial Day holiday, I went fishing at a farm pond known to harbor the South's favorite freshwater game species: *micropterus salmoides*, the largemouth bass. Largemouth are voracious and fierce, which goes a long way toward accounting for their popularity among anglers. The fastidiousness of the trout fisherman is wasted on largemouth, especially in the spring, when warmer water temperatures and the exertions of the spawn incline them to attack almost anything dangled in front of their faces. "But," as Havilah Babcock noted, "bass fishermen can be dumb too, which sort of balances the books and explains why they sometimes catch each other."[3]

Encouraged by this insight, I loaded my rods and tackle box into the truck, together with Jeb, my bird dog, an enthusiastic fellow idiot, and set out after Sunday mass to join another clergyman-angler seeking refreshment at the farm pond.

Fishing is usually slow in the heat of midafternoon. And so it was last Sunday. We caught a few in the shade of some willows, along a hog wire fence that spring rains had caused to jut out

3. Babcock, *My Health*, 79.

improbably a few yards into the pond. But for the most part, the heat lay heavy, and the fish weren't biting.

Having been at this game for many years, I should know better, and yet I always sink into a mild depression as the afternoon wears on. But as the sun touches the horizon and the temperature drops just perceptibly, the first frogs begin to croak, and the waders and shorebirds begin to flutter about, positioning themselves a little more strategically, and the casual angler does well to shake-off the afternoon's torpor and attend to his business.

So we did, and our attention was rewarded by an uptick in the action. The *pièces de résistance* were two truly enormous bass that my companion landed in quick succession, each of which I estimated to be over seven pounds. As the light faded, we fell back to the tailgate and toasted the outcome with a couple of cold beers, as thunderclouds rolled over the horizon in the distance. Lightening, too, loves the twilight.

As we sat on the tailgate, watching the storm clouds on the horizon, the lightening was constant, yet there was no thunder, and the clouds seemed stationary, locked over the monoculture and suburban sprawl in the distance to the east, the graveyard of north Texas's blackland prairie. We were again on the edge of something exceeding our competence, a patchwork of boundaries. Psalm 102 hung somewhere beyond the borders of my consciousness: "They all shall wax old as doth a garment; and as a vesture shalt thou change them, and they shall be changed."

5

THE VERNAL TRANSGRESSION
OF BOUNDARIES

ONE OF MY FAVORITE places to visit in the spring is a creek running through a farm at the precise point where geology has dictated that man should stop growing cotton and start ranching cattle, where the Ozan Formation abuts the Austin Chalk, and the West truly begins. The natural elements of this geologic border are something to behold. The creek is clear and cold, with a limestone bottom, and hemmed in by virgin hardwoods. Around the periphery native bluestems and switchgrass riot with the wildflowers amid stands of post oak and the occasional bois d'arc.

Man has an innate propensity to seek and to test his limits and the limits of his world. Yet some boundaries simply cannot be crossed. Wittgenstein urged his readers to consider the eye's relation to the visual field: "Where in the world is a metaphysical subject to be noted? You say that this case is altogether like that of the eye and the field of sight. But you do not really see the eye."[1] And death, the absolute limit of life, is like that: "Death is not an event of life . . . Our life is endless in the way that our visual field is without limit."[2]

---

1. Wittgenstein, *Tractatus*, 5.633.
2. Wittgenstein, *Tractatus*, 6.4311.

We grope our way in the darkness toward, one hopes, the light and the life. As odd as it seems, it is hard for me to see a prairie after spring rain without thinking of the great liturgical scholar Aidan Kavanagh's poignant description of a baptismal liturgy of the fourth century. He describes an aged bishop leading the newly baptized from the semi-darkness of the baptistery to the church door:

> There he bangs on the closed doors with his cane: they are flung open, the endless vigil is halted, and the baptismal party enters as all take up the hymn, 'Christ is risen . . . .' which is all but drowned out by the ovations that greet Christ truly risen in his newly-born ones. As they enter, the fragrance of chrism fills the church: it is the Easter-smell, God's grace olfactorily incarnate. The pious struggle to get near the newly baptized to touch their chrismed hair and rub its fragrance on their own faces.[3]

I have been struck by the etymology of the word "Lent" ever since I first encountered it. It comes from the Anglo-Saxon word for the spring season—"lencten"— and is related to the word "long," having to do with the "lengthening" of the daylight hours after the winter solstice. Light and warmth return to the world, and as Prudentius wrote of the dawn, so we may say of the spring:

> Earth's gloom flees broken and dispersed,
> By the sun's piercing shafts coerced:
> The daystar's eyes rain influence bright
> And colours glimmer back to sight.[4]

We tend to think of Lent as a time of fasting and self-denial, and so it is. But it is appropriately accompanied by an expectant, spiritual joy, because it is oriented toward the Easter dawn, and even during Lent, the soul rightly revels in its expectation. Such

---

3. Aidan Kavanagh, (lecture, Theology Institute held at Holy Cross Abbey, Canon City, CO, August 1997).

4. Dearmer, "Hymn 54," lines 5–8.

considerations led the priest-poet George Herbert to welcome the "deare *feast* of Lent"[5](italics added).

The vernal continuum of Lent-Easter is the corporate living out of the Lord's words to his disciples: "Unless a grain of wheat falls into the earth and dies, it remains alone; but if it dies, it bears much fruit" (John 12:24). And the natural order, being the most primordial of God's temporal utterances, responds and corresponds: "O Lord my God, great are the wondrous works which thou hast done, like as be also thy thoughts, which are to us-ward" (Psalm 40:5). Seeds that have fallen into the soil begin to sprout and grow, and the face of the earth is renewed by the manifold glories of the flowering plants. "The earth produces of itself, first the blade, then the ear, then the full grain in the ear" (Mark 4:28).

Biblical commentators down the centuries have made much of Easter being on the "eighth day," and thus fulfilling God's purposes in creation when he said, "Let the earth put forth vegetation, plants yielding seed, and fruit trees bearing fruit in which is their seed, each according to its kind, upon the earth" (Genesis 1:11).

In its broadest construal, time, itself a created reality, underwrites the orientation of all things toward their destinies, what in the unfashionable terms of Aristotelian metaphysics are called "final causes." "Therefore the seed is a starting-point and is productive of what comes from it."[6]

Late winter's dormant destinies are disclosed by the spring. The margins and medians of Texas highways, the little "prairie remnants" accidentally preserved on the edges of cultivated or developed land, the establishment of rights-of-way for railroad tracks or power lines are all redolent of resurrection at Easter. All bear witness that "if these were silent, the very stones would cry out" (Luke 19:40). Mother Nature sings her Te Deum at the resurrection of her Lord. "The glorious company of the angiosperms praise Thee!"

In my part of Texas, the ubiquitous blue bonnets, Indian paintbrush, pink evening primrose, prairie verbena, asters in their

5. Herbert, "Lent," line 1.
6. Aristotle, *Parts of Animals*, 29.

myriads glimmer back to sight. It delights me to see this vast army of witnesses each spring, and I find myself seeking wild and semi-wild places to watch the wakeful glimmering.

There is something compelling about borders, something evocative of life and movement. Nor ought we to forget that movement is a sign of life. Seeds themselves must, in the process of their sprouting and growth, transgress the border of the ground from underneath, feeling their way in the darkness toward the light, and so attain their prescribed statures. Yet the Lord sets boundaries for his creatures, great and small. His words to the seas are apt: "Thus far shall you come, and no farther" (Job 38:11).

The earth herself enacts the baptismal liturgy in prototype each spring. My piety leads me to get near and to see, to absorb the fragrance of renewal, mindful of Paul's admonition that our failure to heed the lessons of nature leaves us without excuse (Romans 1). The lessons seem to me to be especially urgent given the gathering late winter darkness of our time and place. As Havel said:

> We must draw our standards from our natural world, heedless of ridicule, and reaffirm its denied validity. We must honor with the humility of the wise the limits of that natural world and the mystery which lies beyond them, admitting that there is something in the order of being which evidently exceeds all our competence.[7]

---

7. Havel, "Politics and Conscience," 267.

6

POLITICS AND NATURE

The Birds of the Air Will Tell You

I OFTEN HAVE THE feeling that we in America are now living in some kind of in-between time, the end of something old or the beginning of something new. Or both. Life in such "spaces" can provoke anxiety, making one feel as though one were subject to forces and sociopolitical shifts much larger than oneself, and well beyond one's control.

Such thoughts and feelings befit the sacramental character of late summer. Here in south Georgia, we recently had several consecutive days of almost pleasant weather: early mornings one would be tempted to call "cool," and afternoons, if one were sitting in the shade and there were a little breeze, were right on the cusp of pleasant. Cloudless sulphur butterflies have appeared in numbers betokening change, with southerly migrants joining year-round residents in little dancing swarms of neon.

As a casual monitor of bird activity, I've noticed that patterns are shifting ever so slightly in that kingdom too. The pileated woodpeckers in the park, where I take Jeb for his daily romp, seem a little more agitated, vocalizing and flitting between the pines, after having spent the last few months in a more staid frame of mind. Cardinals have returned to the backyard, and a pair of bluebirds, for reasons unknown, have been poking around the bluebird box again, which sat on its pole, forlorn in the baking sun, since its former residents abandoned it in the spring.

Of course mourning doves are back in force on power lines, and a few have found their way into my stewpot since the opening day of dove season at the beginning of September. I even flushed a covey of bobwhite quail out in the woods the other day. The last time I paid attention, or had the audacity to venture that far from air-conditioning, they were paired up in fence rows, or whistling singly somewhere in the pines. And did I discern a flock of sandhill cranes croaking south through the stratosphere a week or so ago?

On the other hand, the brown thrashers in my backyard act as though nothing's happening. There are two of them. They were ornery in the spring, ornery through the summer, and they're ornery now. Nothing seems to change for them. Apparently they have no intention of going anywhere. They poke around between a row of monkey grass along the property boundary and some native wildflowers (asters, echinacea, and milkweed) we planted for pollinators beneath the bluebird box. One of them is usually scowling at me as I pull into the driveway, before it disappears, with an air of indignation, into the lower branches of our fig tree as I turn into the carport.

And the heat has returned, all but erasing the memory of that pleasant streak that raised my hopes a couple of weeks ago. The forecast is appalling—mid 90s at best—for as far as my smart-phone's weather oracle can scry into the future.

Yet my intuition remains—something's up. The signs of change predominate among the conflicting signals. The natural world seems to be an icon of the news cycle, where on one level nothing ever seems to change, despite the scattered chirps of revolution. If only the birds could speak! But in a certain sense they do. Scripture insists on this point too. Consider Job 12:7–10:

> But ask the beasts, and they will teach you;
> the birds of the air, and they will tell you;
> or the plants of the earth, and they will teach you;
> and the fish of the sea will declare to you.

Who among all these does not know
that the hand of the LORD has done this?
In his hand is the life of every living thing
and the breath of all mankind.

He is the Lord of heaven *and* earth. A merciful, albeit often in-
scrutable, wisdom and benevolence enfolds the entire expanse of
creation, encompassing every corner at every scale, visible and
invisible, from the subatomic to the intergalactic. "Before him no
creature is hidden, but all are open and laid bare to the eyes of
him with whom we have to do" (Hebrews 4:13). Nothing is left
out, neither flowers (Luke 12:27), nor birds (Luke 12:24), nor the
vicissitudes of weather and climate (Job 37:1–13), nor the various
departments of our dysfunctional government (1 Peter 2:12–17),
nor you, nor me (Luke 12:28).

It is a source of comfort—or it should be!—to the Christian
that he with whom we have to do sits on his throne with sovereign
attention, that the whole cosmic drama is resolving toward a grand
reconciliation with its creator through the cross of Jesus (Colos-
sians 1:19–20). And through it all our task remains the same:
fidelity.

7

THE FALL

ANGLO-AMERICAN FOLKLORE HAS DESIGNATED October's full moon the "hunter's moon," much as September's is called the harvest moon. They mark the arrival and deepening of autumn.

Over the past month or so, the polar jet stream has made its first chilly incursions into my part of Texas. I have turned the air-conditioning off in the house and opened the windows. Evenings have been delicious and mornings crisp.

My daily walk follows a course beneath live oaks, pecans, sweet gums, and a series of four bur oaks—my favorites. (I try hard not to notice non-native ornamental trees.) The nuts have begun to drop, crunching underfoot, making a mess of the sidewalks. Most days I pick up a few pecans and eat them as I walk. This provokes indignation from the squirrels. They run up and down the trees and chatter at me, the thief.

Following their designated forms and ends, inbuilt by the divine wisdom, which "reaches from one end to another, rightly and sweetly ordering all things,[1]" the flora and fauna are preparing for the coming cold. Migratory birds are on the move. Recently, on a walk in the countryside, it thrilled me to hear the rush of wings from blue-winged teal and starlings as they swooped overhead.

1. Gavitt, *Prayer Book*, 312.

Without the city noise, you can actually hear their wings beat. Josef Pieper wrote:

> Leisure is a form of silence, of that silence which is the prerequisite of the apprehension of reality. . . . For leisure is a receptive attitude of mind, a contemplative attitude, and it is not only the occasion but also the capacity for steeping oneself in the world of creation.[2]

By the middle of December, it will be cold, and the natural world will have quieted down. During the spring and summer, all is a riot in woods and fields. From the microbial level and on up the ladder of being, everything is on the move, creeping and eating and singing, bearing and being born. But during winter, all is calm, all is quiet. It is no coincidence that Christians sing "Silent Night" on Christmas Eve, a few short days after the winter solstice.

I make a concerted effort to spend my days-off outdoors, and I enjoy it most when the days are cold. I love to hunt and fish, but these activities are really more occasions for something else: for looking at the natural world and trying to understand it and, by trying to understand it, trying to understand something of what is above, and behind, and beyond it.

That I enjoy this seeing and seeking-to-understand has been a consolation during the first part of autumn, because dove season has been a bust in my corner of the world. Two weeks ago, I set up my decoys, loaded my shotgun, and sat next to Jeb against a hackberry tree by a field of cut milo. In two hours, we saw one single dove fly into a mesquite thicket on the other side of the field, well out of range. But the sun lay beautifully across the gentle contours of the land. Meadowlarks and killdeer gleaned among the browning stalks; a kestrel amused himself ambushing grasshoppers, and much to my surprise and delight (confirmed by my binoculars), a bald eagle was riding thermals in the distance.

Pieper writes, "We may read in the first chapter of Genesis that God 'ended his work which he had made' and 'behold, it was very good.' In leisure, man too celebrates the end of his work by

---

2. Pieper, *Leisure*, 46.

allowing his inner eye to dwell for a while upon the reality of the Creation. He looks and he affirms: it is good.[3]"

Seeing that the created world is good is an aspect of our likeness to God. We participate in a divine activity when we are at rest, still, and silent; or rather, being still and silent is a material condition for participating in this divine work, seeing what God has made, apprehending its goodness.

The natural world itself reflects this. The litter of pecans and acorns on the ground marks the coming end of the warm season's labor—eating and singing and reproduction, photosynthesis and metabolism. The hardwood seeds that wind up in the ground will absorb nutrients from the soil during the winter stillness, like students in a catechetical school (*scholē* in Greek means "leisure") waiting to be baptized by spring rains and illuminated by the all-conquering sun's ascendancy at the vernal equinox. Wendell Berry has written:

> The ecological teaching of the Bible is simply inescap-able: God made the world because He wanted it made. He thinks the world is good, and He loves it. It is His world; He has never relinquished title to it. And He has never revoked the conditions, bearing on His gift to us of the use of it, that oblige us to take excellent care of it. If God loves the world, then how might any person of faith be excused for not loving it or justified in destroying it?[4]

Christianity in America has had a propensity to cede its authority to the liberal order. This was less noticeable before the middle of the twentieth century, when the ethical sphere of liberalism was itself shaped by Christian commitments. But now that faith is waning, incompatibilities and divided loyalties are bubbling increasingly to the surface of American life. Before we are anything else, Christians are Republicans or Democrats and, above all, consumers. The proof lies in an honest assessment of how willing you would be to move houses in order to integrate your family more fully into the life of your church, in comparison with how

3. Pieper, *Leisure*, 49.
4. Berry, *What Are People For?*, 98.

willing you would be to move houses to make your retirement goals more attainable.

Similarly, the degradation of the natural world was less noticeable when the world's population was smaller and per capita energy needs were a fraction of what they are now. But it is ever more difficult to ignore, as many have noted, the loss of biodiversity that has accompanied human population growth and, as Radner writes,

> changes to the earth's atmosphere, the distribution of water on the surface of the earth, chemical compositions of water and soil, structures of subsoil layers, and so on. These changes correlate with the shifting distribution of life on the earth, and the expansion and activities of human beings have caused them.[5]

The concentration of human populations in cities, which began in western Europe in the twelfth century and has now frenetically accelerated globally, means that many people live their lives almost entirely cutoff from the primary realities of nature and of natural processes. As the poet Gerard Manley Hopkins noted: "All is seared with trade; bleared, smeared with toil; / And wears man's smudge and shares man's smell.[6]" It is extremely difficult to see and understand the need for pollinators and the habitats that sustain them when all one knows of one's food is that it comes from a supermarket.

Life inside the bubble of liberal institutions and markets hobbles our ability to participate in a divine work, to see the world as it is, and to see that it is very good. Christians must therefore find opportunities for leisure, in the way that Pieper meant, leisure as a form of "that silence which is the prerequisite of the apprehension of reality."[7] Seeking these opportunities is not a matter of "self-care" or relaxation. Teresa of Avila spoke of the "determined

---

5. Radner, *No Safe Place*, para. 8.

6. Hopkins, "God's Grandeur," In *Poems and Prose*, lines 6–7.

7. Pieper, *Leisure*, 46.

determination"[8] necessary to remain still and quiet, susceptive of God's initiative. This is in fact "our bounden duty and service,"[9] a form of counter-witness, of subversion and sabotage in enemy occupied territory. And it presupposes the courage to apprehend that our society is, as often as not, about the unwitting task of wrecking the good reality we are no longer able to see. "Woe to you! for you are like graves which are not seen, and men walk over them without knowing it" (Luke 11:44). Sacrificial cults always hide their victims from themselves.

Duck season is about to open. I have spent the last month or two studying migration patterns, reading the reports of wildlife biologists about spring breeding patterns and rainfall in latitudes thousands of miles from my home. I have been visiting nearby lakes and streams and taking note of who is passing through—pintails, gadwalls, and mallards—and wondering at the genius, always one step beyond what is empirically verifiable, the traces of the Choreographer of this dance. When I pull the trigger on my shotgun and see a duck fold and fall, when the hunt becomes the kill, it will be a small moment in a process of seeing and seeking-to-understand, a process that stretches from spring rains to thanks returned after a satisfying midwinter meal, and back again.

8. Teresa of Avila, *The Way*, 89.
9. Episcopal Church, *Common Prayer*, 333.

8

CIRCLES OF DISTURBANCE

I LOVE SQUIRREL HUNTING, and I go as often as I can. Oddly enough, I haven't killed a squirrel in years. That doesn't matter to me. If I killed one, I would eat it gratefully. But what I like most about squirrel hunting is being in the hardwood forests where squirrels live. In northeast Texas, hardwood forests lie mostly along riparian corridors, and my favorite place to go is just such a corridor of oaks and pecans and cottonwoods running along a clear, limestone-bottomed creek. I occasionally see squirrels there, and somewhat less occasionally, I will shoot at one. But what I really love is settling in at the base of a stately red oak and just looking and listening.

Getting to my spot requires some effort. As you come to the edge of the woods, there is a little ravine to cross and an old barbed wire fence. The brush is thick along the edge of the woods, and there are plenty of briars and vines that reach out to grab shirts and snatch hats. During the fall and winter, the ground is littered with leaves that rustle and crunch under foot. I like to think that I can move silently through the woods like a Caddo warrior, but that isn't true. I am an uncommonly large, city-dwelling white boy, and I can't get to my spot by the creek without a good deal of blunder, clatter, and imprecation.

If you want to see wildlife in the wild, blunder, clatter, and imprecation are not your allies. The Lord said to Noah, "The fear of you and the dread of you shall be upon every beast of the earth, and upon every bird of the air, upon everything that creeps on the ground and all the fish of the sea" (Genesis 9:2). I have confirmed this by experience. If you want to see wildlife, it is best that they not know that you are there.

With that in mind, I wear earth-toned clothes, and once I have blundered into my spot, I get as comfortable and as quiet as I can. I sit still and wait. At first there will be only the sound of the wind in the trees and the water over the rock, but after half an hour or so, animals will reemerge from their hiding places. Birds perch and chirp. Voles scuttle in the leaf litter. If I'm lucky, something higher up the chain of being will manifest itself—a deer, a turkey . . . or a squirrel.

I once listened to a lecture by an outdoors professional about how to move through the woods. He laid out the foregoing dynamic in terms of concentric circles surrounding a person moving through the woods. If, like me, you are a blunderer, then the circle closest to you is the "circle of perception," the immediate vicinity that you see and engage with as you clamber over fallen logs and curse the briars attempting to filch your hat. Beyond that circle of perception, extending far beyond what you can perceive, is a "circle of disturbance," the area within which the fear of you and the dread of you has fallen upon the animal kingdom. The disturbance ripples outward beyond what you immediately create, as disturbed animals in turn disturb others.

A few years ago, an article in the New York Times reported:

> Studies in recent years by many researchers . . . have shown that animals such as birds, mammals and even fish recognize the alarm signals of other species. Some can even eavesdrop on one another across classes. Red-breasted nuthatches listen to chickadees. Dozens of birds listen to tufted titmice, who act like the forest's crossing guards. Squirrels and chipmunks eavesdrop on birds, sometimes adding their own thoughts. In Africa,

vervet monkeys recognize predator alarm calls by superb starlings.[1]

Animal "language" is far more nuanced than we knew, distinguishing between various kinds of threats and their locations. "Don't get eaten by that lurching human who has just twisted his ankle!" peeps the warbler to the chipmunk.

It's important to realize that the size of one's circle of disturbance is inversely proportional to the size of one's circle of perception. If you are only aware of what is immediately around you—the root on which you have just twisted your ankle—then you will be more apt to frighten animals with your ruckus. But as your attention extends farther out, you naturally slow down and move more quietly, and the area within which your movements elicit attention (and alarm) shrinks back towards yourself.

There is a spiritual lesson in all of this. God is the archetype of stillness and silence, and this divine stillness and silence is manifested most fully within this world on the cross—the still silence of our crucified Lord who sees all and disturbs none. It is then no coincidence that "before him no creature is hidden, but all are open and laid bare to the eyes of him with whom we have to do" (Hebrews 4:13).

When our attention is focused narrowly on ourselves and the things and people in our immediate vicinity, we blunder heedlessly through life, creating a great deal of psychic commotion and a large circle of spiritual disturbance. But by slowing down, becoming still and quiet, allowing our attention to range further afield, encompassing all things, and ultimately expanding beyond the horizon of all things, reaching out to Him "who is above all and through all and in all," (Ephesians 4:6), we will discover real stillness, the divine peace that passes all understanding. Which is to say that our spiritual circle of disturbance will have shrunk to nothing, engulfed by Calvary when it is set up in our hearts.

---

1. Solomon, "When Birds Squawk," lines 20–25.

9

ROD AND GUN

To me, September 1 means the beginning of the end of summer. It's the opening day of dove season, and the beginning of the hunting season more broadly construed. It marks the time when I begin to focus less on rod and more on gun. This year on September 1, I was in a sunflower field in south Georgia. It was obscenely hot, a south Georgia kind of hot, where you're teased by passing clouds and momentary breezes, but you mostly sit and swelter. I was posted up next to a hay bale and kept adjusting myself to take advantage of the few inches of shade it afforded at midday.

I was desperately attempting to insert the lower part of my left leg into the shadow under the curve of the hay bale's fat middle, adjusting and readjusting my stool with that end in view, when the hunter immediately to my left, about thirty yards away, shouted "Bird!" to the hunter about thirty yards to the left of him. I squinted just in time to see the dove diving toward a decoy hanging from a mock power line. I saw a burst of feathers as the bird crumpled, just as the sound of two shots reached my ears: "Boom! Boom!"

And so it was on. Birds came in by twos and threes pretty steadily from the surrounding pines for the next hour or so—and thank God for that, since it was harder to focus on the blistering sun when all my psychic energy was absorbed in missing shots. With dove, the ratio of shots-taken to birds-in-the-bag is generally considered to be a more important and revealing metric than simply *how many* birds you kill. In a field such as this one, any fair-to-middling shooter can take a limit, and all twenty or so of the hunters present did in fact shoot limits. The question is: how many shells did you fire to take that limit? The answer, in my case, is more than I care to disclose. I will offer as an excuse the fact that I was getting used to a new shotgun—and the fact that said shotgun was a 20-gauge over-under, i.e., and not a three-shot, 12-gauge meat collector. But the afternoon also vindicated Nash Buckingham's observation in 1947 that dove shooting "offers more challenges to the finer phases of field gunning than any other sporting species."[1] Quite.

That first dove was followed quickly by a steady trickle of his friends during the ensuing hour or so. Then two things happened simultaneously. It started to drizzle—one of those late summer drizzles in which the sun is still shining in a partly cloudy sky, but the little shower was enough to take the edge off the blistering heat. Seemingly at the same moment, the sunflower field exploded with doves. The birds were corkscrewing this way and that as the report of shotguns erupted from all sides. The birds looked like bees swarming over the tops of the sunflowers, arching and buzzing all over the place in twos and threes, fours and fives, groups that bisected and trisected each other, joined together and separated, a chaotic scene with so many targets that I had to remind myself to aim at individual birds. My natural instinct in such situations is to aim at groups rather than picking out a single bird, and this leads only to misses or at best accidental hits.

I focused my attention and my aim improved sufficiently for me to finish my limit of fifteen birds in the next twenty minutes or so, cooled by the light rain and energized by this very fine phase of field gunning.

I can count on my fingers the number of dove hunts that I've been on when the birds were as plentiful and the shooting as fast-paced as it was on September 1 of this year. All of the guns had collected their limits and were out of the field in a little over an

---

1. Buckingham, *The Best*, 188.

hour and a half, nursing cold beers by the tailgates of trucks once the shooting stopped, and by turns complimenting or ribbing each other on the day's marksmanship, comparing shotguns, laughing and lying and declaiming, comparing this hunt to other opening days in years or decades past, remembering long gone companions from those other hunts: brothers, friends, dads, and dogs.

It was the kind of dove hunt that I love. Good shooting and bag limits all around are merely the catalyst for what's much more important: the conviviality, the friendships made or renewed. But the abundance of birds plays its part too, and hunters cannot take them for granted. In the early part of the twentieth century, the future of wing shooting didn't look bright. Year-round shooting of doves and other species, a lack of bag limits, and the inability of natural resource managers to enforce regulations, led to sharp and noticeable declines in bird numbers. The lack of a federal regulatory framework had made these problems possible. And it was forward-thinking sportsmen who understood the dynamics of the issues at play and what was at stake. Hunters like Nash Buckingham, Ding Darling, George Bird Grinnell, and many others, saw what was happening and were willing to get their hands dirty, advocating with their elected representatives and crafting the conservation policies that would lead to the recovery of mourning doves and many other species. It is thanks to those men and that work that experiences like this year's opening day are still possible.

One of my fondest desires is that future generations of hunters and anglers might be able to have the same kinds of experiences I have had in the field and on the water. I want them to be able to stand around docks and the tailgates of trucks long after I'm gone, to be able to crack open a cold beer with their friends, and not just remember how it used to be, but give thanks for how it has remained. For that to happen, our world needs conscientious hunters and anglers. We need hunters and anglers willing to insist that the future of hunting and fishing not be sold out for the short-term economic interests of a few, to insist on resilient and intelligent laws that will ensure that our fish and game populations remain abundant for us and for future generations.

10

THE SEA

What can the sea tell her,
    That she does not now know, and know how to bear?
She knows, as the sea, that what came will recur,
    And detached in that wisdom, is aware
How grain by slow grain, the last sun heat from sand is
expended on night air.
Bare flesh of an old foot knows that much, as she stands
there.[1]

                —Robert Penn Warren

WITTGENSTEIN WROTE IN THE Tractatus: "To view the world sub specie aeterni is to view it as a whole—a limited whole. Feeling the world as a limited whole—it is this that is mystical."[2] When seen from a sufficient height, human life and human ingenuity recede into insignificance. During the Holocene Wet Phase, much of the Sahara Desert was a verdant savannah, teeming with animal and human life. During the Cretaceous Period, Texas was at the bottom of the sea.

When I was in the discernment process for ordination, I recall being asked on a psychological evaluation whether I was afraid of deep water. The question stopped me. On the one hand, I

1. Warren, "Foreign Shore," In *Selected Poems,* lines 25–30.
2. Wittgenstein, *Tractatus,* 6.45.

57

didn't want to be disqualified due to insanity or irrational phobias, but on the other hand, I had resolved going into the exam to be scrupulously honest. The question conjured images of floating in the open ocean at night, with thousands of feet of dark water and who-knows-what between me and the ocean floor. I answered that yes, I am afraid of deep water.

Gazing out of the window of an airplane on a recent flight to Bermuda, I thought about deep water. The waters of the open ocean are dark, even in broad sunshine, and incomprehensibly vast. Seen from an airplane, ocean islands, and all the human doings that they sustain, seem insignificant and fragile surrounded by the limitless blue. Geologically minor jostlings of the earth's crust can cause immense disruptions to human life, calamities for coastal and island communities, as happened during the Tōhoku earthquake and tsunami of 2011, which led to the reactor meltdowns at the Fukushima Daiichi Nuclear Power Plant. Nearly sixteen thousand people lost their lives. Most of them drowned.

Yet as I stared out the window of another airplane, flying from Texas to Wisconsin several years ago, I saw the entire central part of a continent brought under the plow, a checkerboard of farm roads and telltale signs of pivot irrigation. Mankind is small compared with Tellus Mater, but we are many (Mark 5:9).

> God said to them, "Be fruitful and multiply, and fill the earth and subdue it; and have dominion over the fish of the sea and over the birds of the air and over every living thing that moves upon the earth" (Genesis 1:28).

The stewardship of the earth and the seas, and of the resources that come from them, is a matter of obedience. Yet we often seem to be failing, abetted in this failure by economic systems that incentivize mere exploitation. Furthermore, the exponential growth of the human population over the past century, which shows no signs of slowing, is putting immense pressure on wildlife and other natural resources. Stock assessments of the Gulf of Mexico red snapper fishery indicated that by 1990 the fishery's spawning potential was just 2.6 percent of what it would be with no fishing pressure—an insufficient ratio that can neither sustain the fishery itself nor the human communities that rely on it.

When it comes to the dominion mandate from Genesis, laissez-faire policies are no longer adequate, if they ever were. Creative solutions across the board are necessary—solutions that evince due humility in the face of the vastness of earth, sky, and sea, and more particularly, solutions that evince due humility before our common Lord. But dominion must also defer to the dignity of work; create, sustain, and reward solidarity between rich and poor; recognize the family as a fundamental economic unit; and foster an ethic of responsible stewardship and simple agency at the most local levels possible. Perhaps most importantly, new solutions must elicit from man a *delight* in the primary realities of creation, and not merely habits of exploitative utility. Delight in creation is a facet of our likeness to God (Genesis 1:31), and its abatement therefore is a symptom of sin.

When ancient peoples looked out at the sea, they recognized a vast and ungovernable power, at once life-giving and lethal, a source of food and the abode of dragons. One thinks of Leviathan, Behemoth, Rahab, or Jonah and the whale.

In February of 2007, fishermen in the Ross Sea off of Antarctica caught a squid that weighed over a thousand pounds. It was a colossal squid (*Mesonychoteuthis hamiltoni*), a species affected by an evolutionary phenomenon called abyssal gigantism. Colossal squid can grow over forty feet long and have the largest eyes of any known animal, sometimes over a foot in diameter. Yet biologists estimate that, due to a very slow metabolism, these enormous creatures require only about an ounce of food per day, suggesting that they spend most of their time lurking in ambush, like the "young lion" of Psalm 17. They have been known to attack sperm whales and, according to maritime legends, even ships.

As I was recently examining a depth chart of Bermuda, I noticed that the Atlantic drops precipitously to over a thousand fathoms (over a mile deep) a short distance from shore, showing Bermuda to be the peak of a steep volcanic mountain. The deepest part of the Atlantic is the Milwaukee Deep, north of Puerto Rico, at over twenty-seven thousand feet. "There go the ships, and there is that Leviathan: whom thou hast made to take his pastime therein" (Psalm 104:26). What else lurks in those waters? What of human artifice, what human lives, have been lost in them down the centuries? What lies at the bottom, and why does it lie there?

Yet every morning I read in Psalm 95: "The sea is his, for he made it." And as the Lord reminded the precocious Job:

> Where were you when I laid the foundation of the earth?
> Tell me, if you have understanding.
> Who determined its measurements—surely you know!
> Or who stretched the line upon it?
> On what were its bases sunk,
> or who laid its cornerstone,
> when the morning stars sang together,
> and all the sons of God shouted for joy?
> Or who shut in the sea with doors,
> when it burst forth from the womb;
> when I made clouds its garment,
> and thick darkness its swaddling band,
> and prescribed bounds for it,
> and set bars and doors,
> and said, 'Thus far shall you come, and no farther,
> and here shall your proud waves be stayed'?
> Have you commanded the morning since your days began,
> and caused the dawn to know its place? (Job 38:4–12).

A certain diffidence behooves us in the face of creation's mysteries. It is the task of the natural sciences to interrogate creation, but the relation is properly dialogic. Nor are we, priests and kings of creation, exempt from interrogation. Augustine reports (in Book 10 of the *Confessions*) how earth, sky, and sea bore witness to him, "by their beauty of order,"[3] of the sovereignty of God— "He made us!" they cried with one voice. This led naturally to introspection: "I turned my thoughts into myself and said, 'Who are you?'" Who are we, indeed? Who do we now think we are?

---

3. Augustine, *Confessions*, 183; my translation.

Creation's beauty of form, Augustine says, is visible to all "whose senses are unimpaired."[4]

There are intimations sprinkled throughout the Old Testament that God will subdue the waters of the earth and the overwhelming powers of darkness and death that inhabit them in the cosmologies of ancient peoples, seemingly the residue of the watery, primordial chaos of Genesis 1:2. There are intimations too that as often as not mankind has allied himself with the abyssal darkness, that the subdual of the latter will coincide with our judgment.

In 2016 the National Institutes of Health announced that it would lift a ban on the creation in laboratories of human-animal hybrids, so-called "chimeras," beings that are part pig and part human, for example. And there is no doubt that these things are to be created only to be killed on the altar of "medical research." Cures will be promised—just as Moloch promised to water the crops of the seafaring Carthaginians in exchange for their children's blood. How this new reality does not inspire widespread revulsion is beyond me. It is like the sight of a drowning shorebird, covered in oil. But much worse.

> For behold, the LORD is coming forth out of his place to punish the inhabitants of the earth for their iniquity, and the earth will disclose the blood shed upon her, and will no more cover her slain. In that day the LORD with his hard and great and strong sword will punish Leviathan the fleeing serpent, Leviathan the twisting serpent, and he will slay the dragon that is in the sea" (Isaiah 26:21—27:1).

Ratzinger has suggested in *Jesus of Nazareth* that this is one facet of Jesus' descent into the waters at his baptism, the fulfillment of his promise once and for all to subjugate the roving powers of the formless void.[5] And Jesus himself connects his descent into the waters of the earth with his descent into the earth itself at his death (Mark 10:39). Yet judgment coincides with mercy. The

4. Augustine, *Confessions*, 184.

5. Ratzinger, *Jesus of Nazareth*, 19–20.

ungovernable powers of the world will be brought into subjection and, in the same motion, the meek of the earth will be delivered:

> "Thou smotest the heads of Leviathan in pieces: thou gavest him to be meat for the people in the wilderness" (Psalm 74:15).

11

GRASS

This is the most beautiful place on earth.
There are many such places.[1]

I HAVE A LIST of favorite places. Almost all of them are notable for the extent to which they have not been disturbed by man. Within the last year or so I have added to this list—and it currently resides near the top—a small patch of prairie on the Texas side of the Texas-Oklahoma border, along the shore of the aptly, if unimaginatively, named Lake Texoma.

Immediately there is an irony to be noticed. Lake Texoma is itself a grand, artificial disturbance, created in 1939 when the US Army Corps of Engineers built a dam at the confluence of the Red River and the Washita River. The lake inundated ninety thousand acres of land and swallowed up several towns. Remnants of some of the lost towns were exposed in 2011 when the water level receded in the face of a protracted drought.

Dammed rivers are not the only aspect of our having filled and subdued the earth hereabout. And droughts are a symptom of other problems. When settlers first arrived in the middle part of what was still becoming the United States, they encountered a sea of grass, covering almost four-hundred thousand square miles,

---

1. Abbey, *Desert Solitaire*, 1.

from southern Canada to northern Mexico. It came to be that way when, about eleven thousand years ago, glaciers withdrew to the north, leaving behind a layer of till onto which winds dropped silt and organic matter. Natural wildfires and vast herds of buffalo ensured that trees and shrubs were kept to a minimum. One secret of the prairie's success lies in the fact that 80 percent of its biomass lies underground, in the root structures of grasses and forbs. Fire and roving herds of large grazing animals are integral components of grassland ecology.

The Blackland Prairie is the name ecologists have given to the ecological region where Dallas now sits. It extended northeast-southwest, from the Red River to near San Antonio, like a finger pointing toward Mexico. It was characterized by tall grasses—big bluestem, little bluestem, Indian grass, and switchgrass, among others—which can grow over six feet tall. It was bordered to the east by the pine forests of east Texas and to the west by an ecological complex known colloquially as the Cross Timbers region (historically characterized by shorter grasses interspersed with stands of blackjack and post oak).

European settlers didn't like wildfires, and as they moved in, they put the fires out. Apparently they also didn't like the buffalo. Between 1872 and 1874, eight hundred fifty thousand buffalo hides were shipped out of Dodge City alone. One man, "Buffalo Bill" Cody, shot 4,280 buffalo (he counted) in the course of twelve months. In 1837, John Deere invented the steel plow, and by 1855 he had sold over ten thousand of them. The invention is commemorated on a historical monument in Middlebury, Vermont, where Deere learned blacksmithing. The monument calls his invention "The plow that broke the plains." And so it did. By 1930 the Blackland Prairie was pretty much gone, together with most of the rest of the plains' grasslands, converted to agriculture or pasture or, lately and especially in north Texas, metrosprawl.

The land has become less resilient in the face of capricious weather. Native prairie plants have deep and extensive root structures in comparison with the monocultures and asphalt that have replaced them. For example, the roots of the compass plant

(*Silphium laciniatum*), a common prairie flower, can reach up to fifteen feet deep. The roots of cotton and wheat typically don't grow much deeper than three feet. Deep roots hold the soil together and hold water in the soil. Without the roots, wind erosion becomes a much bigger problem, as in the Dust Bowl of the 1930s, and water runs off more readily. Shortly before his death in 2013, at the age of ninety-two, the author John Graves remembered listening, as a young man, to farmers on the steps of the Parker County courthouse in Weatherford, Texas: "Hell, I done wore out three farms in my time,"[2] one said. Droughts are more impactful now, and spring storms lead to downstream flooding of the kind we seem to see every year lately in east Texas and Louisiana. Thirteen people were killed by storms and floods in the spring of 2017. In many respects our young land does indeed seem "wore out."

But patches of native prairie remain here and there, along rights-of-way for railroads, highways, and powerlines, or in pockets of land that the march of progress somehow overlooked or forgot. Such an overlooked pocket is my little spot on the south shore of Lake Texoma. It has never been developed, and probably never plowed, and it may well never have been grazed. For the last hundred years or so, it has been in a remote corner of land used as a youth camp, first by the Boy Scouts and then by various churches. Not much before that, judging from the arrowheads and chipped flint that turn up from time to time, it was the home or the hunting grounds of the Caddo or Wichita, or Comanche or Kiowa, or Apache or Osage—likely different groups at different times—stretching back a long time, back indeed to the time of saber-toothed cats and woolly mammoths. I'm not naïve about the ecological impact and caprice of American Indians—in some ways they were just like everyone else. One common hunting practice was to drive whole herds of bison over cliffs, and you might if you could, ask an eighteenth century Apache for his opinion of the Comanche, or vice versa. But, for one thing, there were never nearly as many of them as there are of us. And, as I've said, the prairie was resilient.

2. Weeks, "For Earth Day," para. 5.

My prairie patch in north Texas somehow survived. It sits in the middle of a much larger upland forest in which post oaks predominate. Wet weather creeks drop into widening draws and then into the main body of what used to be the Red River. As you walk through the woods toward the grassland at their center, you notice what's conspicuous—non-native and invasive plants like nandina, a popular ornamental native to Asia. Birds eat the berries and deposit the seeds in the woods. There is also one very hateful Bradford pear, another Asian native. God knows how it got there. But there are conspicuous charmers too—eastern redbuds flash out brightly in early spring, and there's a lovely little possumhaw by a pool at the bottom of a rock ledge. One spring, I inadvertently flushed a pair of mallards from the pool. As they escaped through the trees, I wondered why they had been sitting in this muddy little pool in the forest when ninety thousand acres of open water lie just beyond the trees. They were probably embarrassed lovers.

Two giant sycamore trees keep watch over the entrance to the grassland. I noticed their huge leaves on the ground before I saw the trees a couple hundred yards through the woods. They are easily recognizable because of their flaking bark and mottled upper trunks, and because of their telltale fruit, brown golf balls dangling in the sunlight from slender stems, and not least because they loom head and shoulders above the surrounding landscape. They are protected by a year-round spring that has rendered the ground muddy and the brush thick. Twice I have tried to push through to them. Twice I have been rebuffed by briars and come home with poison ivy.

Emerging from the woods into the grassland is like walking into a new world. I love knowing and saying the names of the grasses and flowers—Indian grass, little bluestem, milkweed, false indigo, yarrow, Indian paintbrush, bushy bluestem, meadow garlic, poppy mallow—and it frustrates me not to know the names of everything. "And whatever the man called every living creature, that was its name" (Genesis 2:19).

There are signs of man-made disturbance too, but they are mercifully few. A four-wheeler track transgresses the property boundary over a downed fence, and there is a half-covered midden formed by the detritus of a campsite, abandoned several decades ago by the looks of it. A more recent campfire ring is tucked behind a stand of eastern red cedar in one corner, and there are discreet piles of beer cans in a few places. But the disturbance really is mild compared with what one typically sees in semi-wildernesses close to civilization.

Scripture seems to take grassland ecology as an icon of transient fragility, standing in contrast to the solidity of the divine word. "The grass withers, the flower fades; but the word of our God will stand for ever" (Isaiah 40:8). Mankind is more like the grass than he is like the word, on account of which, St. James exhorts the rich to boast only in his humiliation, "because like the flower of the grass he will pass away" (James 1:10).

But Scripture also evinces an intuitive knowledge of ecological subtleties, like the trophic levels of the food chain. An abundance of grass means a proportionate abundance of grazing animals, and this in turn constitutes a blessing for the people who rely on the grazing animals for sustenance. Scripture knows this. The Lord "will give grass in your fields for your cattle, and you shall eat and be full" (Deuteronomy 11:15). Pastoral societies understood their place in the natural economy better than we do, and hunter-gatherers understood it better yet. On average about ten percent of the energy of a given level of the food chain is transferred to the one above it. This is why there were fewer wolves than buffalo, and fewer buffalo than forage plants. And at the very bottom of the scale, only about 1 percent of the chemical energy of plants comes from photosynthesized sunlight. Wittgenstein said more than he knew when he wrote that, apart from the resurrection of Christ, "We are in a sort of hell where we can do nothing but dream, roofed in, as it were, and *cut off from heaven*"[3] (italics added). Running the numbers, our bodies are made up of about .001 percent sunlight. Not very much.

3. Wittgenstein, *Culture and Value*, 33.

> The LORD God sent [Adam] forth from the garden of
> Eden, to till the ground from which he was taken. He
> drove out the man; and at the east of the garden of Eden
> he placed the cherubim, and a flaming sword which
> turned every way, to guard the way to the tree of life
> (Genesis 3:23–24).

Are we wearing out the earth's ability to sustain us, tilling the ground into oblivion, coming to the end of some invisible tether? The earth's resources are renewable, it's true. But their renewal is predicated upon man's faithful and prudent stewardship. We have never been good at it, and we appear to be getting worse. We take it for granted that GDP growth is a good thing. But is the growth of the economy the same thing as—or even compatible with—human flourishing in a fundamental way? Can the economy go on growing forever, as our leaders seem to hope, when the earth's resources are finite? The buffalo hunters went about their mad work because they could get rich doing it. Buffalo hide coats became fashionable in Europe in the middle of the nineteenth century. Perhaps this is why Scripture sees the renewal of the face of the earth as God's business (Psalm 104:30). Man prefers cash.

Indeed, very often there is a tacit assumption in the discourse of ecologists that mankind is the problem. I see the impulse in my own thinking too—a propensity to a kind of impulsive conservatism, an urge to stand athwart natural history shouting, "Stop!" How did things stand before the settlement of North America by Europeans, and how might we return things to such a state? Perennial questions. But ecologists tend toward irreligion, as a class, which forestalls appeals to ultimate origins or purposes and blinds them to the truth. In such an ideological landscape, there is no justification for seeing mankind as anything other than one part of nature, and an insignificant part in the grand scheme. The glaciers will probably return in time whether we like it or not.

There is no justification in passing definitive moral judgment on the squandering of our ecological inheritance if we cannot see it as an inheritance to begin with, as something with which we have been entrusted by the One to whom it really belongs, to whom we will have to render an account of our stewardship. Perhaps, in the end, it was Jesus' awareness of the fact "that he had come from God and was going to God," that underwrote his awareness of God having "given all things into his hands" (John 13:3). Including, we may assume, the tallgrass prairie. But we don't see things that way anymore, if we ever really did.

Yet it is only in the knowledge of our ultimate origin, and hence of our journey, and hence, broadly speaking, of our purpose, that the purpose of all the rest comes into view—the right ordering of our symbiosis with the buffalo and the grass and with one another. The fire ring in my prairie, the four-wheeler tracks, the modest little piles of beer cans, the decomposing campsite midden—they *are*, in point of fact, an outrage. Yet a much more profound outrage has been averted, if only for the time being and if only in regard to these few relict acres.

I once showed my prairie to a biologist who specializes in grassland ecology. I wanted to confirm my untutored suspicion that this patch of land was relatively intact and worth preserving. As we emerged from the woods, under the watchful gaze of the sentinel sycamores, she looked around at the Indian grass running down the gentle contours of the land. "Oh my God!" she gasped. "You have something precious here."

12

THE TRINITY RIVER

I OFTEN USED TO spend my days off walking through the roughly ten thousand acres of virgin hardwood forest down by the Trinity River. Although only about four miles from downtown Dallas, it's a world away, mercifully regarded by the city fathers as unfit for agriculture or development as it lies within the river's floodplain. One of my favorite parts of the forest was a stand of Texas buckeyes and bur oaks and pecans, right along the banks of the river. It was gorgeous and riotously lush in the spring, but I liked it best in midwinter when it was bright and quiet and green and gold.

Engagement with the primary reality of creation is a psychic and theological imperative for human beings. In 1753 Benjamin Franklin wrote of how Indian children raised among the English, "taught our language and habituated to our customs,"[1] would never return to civilization once they had the opportunity of spending time among their kin. Conversely, English children raised among the Indians would, upon being ransomed by their white families, escape back into the woods at the first opportunity, "whence there is no reclaiming them." Several decades later, John Hector St. John interviewed two such Europeans who refused to return to civilization. Among the reasons they gave for remaining among the Indians, St. John says, were "the absence of those cares and corroding

1. Founders Online, "Franklin to Collinson," para. 8.

solicitudes"[2] which are the all-encompassing preoccupations of the civilized.

As St. Paul wrote, "Ever since the creation of the world [God's] invisible nature, namely, his eternal power and deity, has been clearly perceived in the things that have been made" (Romans 1:20). Yet how quickly is the vision occluded when it must be glimpsed through layer upon layer of abstraction—books and engines and smart phones—or even when it is arrested and stylized, as in a public park or a garden.

I once sat by the muddy flume of the Trinity, ate my lunch, and thought about God's invisible nature, namely, his eternal power and deity. At its best, theology, unlike the other sciences, has no technical vocabulary. It uses ordinary language—words like "father," "bread," "wine," or "water"—to translate God and the things of God to us. "God" itself is a word we borrowed from the pagans (their word for members of their pantheon). Now it denotes whatever we think most highly of or, in the lexicon of our day's atheistic scientism, whatever we find most incomprehensible and are angriest at. Wittgenstein compared the discipline of philosophy to a sickness of the soul,[3] and to be sure, God is sometimes lost in translation, as though he gets tangled up in our words. Surely our social estrangement from the Spouse of our souls began with, or at least is exacerbated by, our penchant for abstraction, our addiction to it, and the failure of our imagination that has led us to build an artificial universe on the binary foundation of overly simple affirmations and denials, ones and zeros.

The seventeenth century Christian mystic Angelus Silesius wrote:

> To become Nothing is to become God
> Nothing becomes what is before: if you do not become nothing,
> Never will you be born of eternal light.[4]

2. De Crèvecoeur, *Letters*, 213–214.

3. See, for example, Wittgenstein, *Investigations*, 51.

4. Derrida, *On the Name*, 43.

Three centuries after Silesius, in the wake of his mother's death, Jacques Derrida glossed this epigram: "This becoming-self as becoming-God—or Nothing—that is what appears impossible, more than impossible, the most impossible possible, more impossible than the impossible if the impossible is the simple negative modality of the possible."[5] We must take leave of "god" in order to find God. The meek shall inherit the earth.

Sitting by the Trinity that midwinter day, I finished my lunch and tossed an apple core into the river as an alligator gar stirred the silt—the fish and the silt both relics of the early Cretaceous, the time when the earth brought forth flowering plants and God saw that it was good. I thought of Ezekiel 47:12: "And on the banks, on both sides of the river, there will grow all kinds of trees for food."

A pileated woodpecker, arrogant and reclusive, flashed through the branches and began a mad search for bugs in the bark of a hackberry tree. The tree attracts the bugs, but the bugs can kill the tree, so the bird eats the bugs. "God appointed a plant," and "God appointed a worm," (Jonah 4), and God appointed a pileated woodpecker. And the prophet "wrapped his face in his mantle and . . . behold, there came a voice to him, and said, 'What are you doing here?'" (1 Kings 19).

Years ago there was an absurd attempt to make Dallas an inland port. Once a steamship even made it from the Gulf all the way up the Trinity to town. It took about a year of dredging and clearing log jams, and it was never attempted again. But the point had been made: Man can run against creation's current, though the effort exhausts him. But with enough congressional funding, it can be made to work and done regularly. Several years ago I read that the British House of Commons approved the making of laboratory babies from the genes of three parents. I used to be interested in the maddening discourse of theodicy, but I have departed in peace. It is simply a mysterious facet of God's humility that man can thwart his will. They are now building a golf course on several hundred acres in a corner of my forest.

---

5. Derrida, *On the Name*, 43.

So much for moral evil. But what of subrational nature? I once watched in disgust as a seagull pecked a rock dove to death. The seagull stood on top of the dove and pecked at it as the dove flapped helplessly. The gull would pause and strut a few paces away, glance around defiantly, then strut back over to the dove and peck some more. The flapping was reduced to quivering and twitching, and the seagull finally flew off and left the bleeding dove to die.

Many predators are known sometimes to kill seemingly for the sheer joy of it. In 2003 researchers in Canada's Northwest Territories reported finding the carcasses of thirty-four caribou calves, all killed by wolves, spread over a three-kilometer area, most of them entirely uneaten. The suggestion of Genesis is that creation's suffering is somehow man's fault, and this I believe. The very ground—out of which men and seagulls and rock doves and wolves and caribou and poison ivy all grow—is cursed on our account (Genesis 3:17).

But, as Hopkins said, in words that have become a touchstone for me:

> And for all this, nature is never spent;
> There lives the dearest freshness deep down things;
> And though the last lights off the black West went
> Oh, morning, at the brown brink eastward, springs –
> Because the Holy Ghost over the bent
> World broods with warm breast and with ah! bright wings.[6]

It is popularly believed that the Holy Ghost has been given short shrift in Western theology, from Augustine's *De Trinitate* on down to the present. Augustine made much, maybe too much, of a peculiarity of the Latin Vulgate in which man is created "*ad* imaginem Dei"[7] (*toward* the image of God). The idea being that the only word perfectly expressive of God is the word God himself utters, *the* Word, the Son. But the body of man is also created a temple of the Holy Spirit, on account of which we are not our own, but merely stewards of ourselves (1 Corinthians 6:19). What sort of

6. Hopkins, "God's Grandeur," In *Poems and Prose*, lines 9–14.

7. Italics added.

selves ought we therefore to be, sinful and susceptible to sickness as we are?

A cold breeze hovered over the Trinity as I sat next to it that day. Deep called to deep in the murmuring of its eddies. The only signs of civilization were a morass of plastic grocery bags caught in the branches overhanging the river. But for the moment the woods around me were clean and bright. And the Trinity was slowly and inexorably sweeping everything given to it, and the land itself, toward the limitless expanse of the Gulf.

13

BLOOD ON MY HANDS

I HAVE BEEN A hunter for as long as I can remember. As a child this meant squirrel safaris with BB guns or slingshots, "afield" with my friends in backyards and woods accessible by bicycle. More occasionally it meant outings to farms with my uncles and cousins after quail or dove ("buhds" they were called categorically). I learned a lot about the rudiments of adult responsibility from these outings. One could lose an eye to a BB gun or a slingshot (once I very nearly did). It was indelibly impressed upon me that even a single-shot .410 or a .22 rifle was not a toy and could easily kill a person. The cardinal rules of gun safety were drilled and redrilled on each outing. Later I would learn to abstract them and apply them to life more generally. How many life mistakes could I have avoided if I had taken the time and care to be sure of my target and what was beyond it?

A misbegotten and reactionary foray into vegetarianism during high school was inspired by my reading of a letter on the subject by Leo Tolstoy. His argument ran roughly as follows: You know that you can be perfectly healthy without eating meat, so if you eat meat, you are doing it to gratify your appetite at the expense of the lives of animals.[1] That made sense to me, but more significantly, it was a convenient platform for my teenage moralism.

1. Tolstoy, "Letter to Schmitt," 43.

My family had moved by that time to the sprawling metropolis of southeastern Virginia, and hunting opportunities were few and far between. My shotgun was sitting neglected in the closet anyway.

I abandoned vegetarianism in college—forced to do so, I felt, by the lack of options in the college refectory. "Man cannot live by cheese pizza and iceberg lettuce alone," I reasoned with myself. Tolstoy had obviously not been an undergraduate at Sewanee. After quick transgressions with fish and chicken, my gustatory horizons expanded beyond my scruples and once again encompassed hamburgers and pepperoni. Circumstances coalesced, as they will, and I returned to the field, and that with increasing frequency as the years have gone by. I have done my share for land management by removing from the landscape quite a few of the twenty-first century's great, invasive destroyer: the wild hog. Eastern and Rio Grande turkeys have found their way into my bag, and I have taken many species of big game across two continents. But my favorite quarry remains "buhds"—typically dove, duck, and every so often, the quail that have been rapidly disappearing, along with their habitat, from their historic range in eastern and central North America.

I am haunted to this day by Tolstoy's logic, but the distinctions have grown ever subtler in my mind and seasoned by Richard Hooker's "three-legged stool." God gave animals to man for food after the flood (Genesis 9:3), and we know that God came to earth and tucked into at least fish (John 21:9–13) and lamb (Luke 22:8–15). Jase Robertson once mentioned on *Duck Dynasty* (a tv show and a phenomenon that fascinates me) that he prefers not to eat meat that he hasn't killed himself. That sentiment haunts me too, and it has to some extent exorcised the ghost of Tolstoy from my consciousness. It injects into the economy of food an element of personal responsibility for the usually unconsidered bloodletting and violence that makes eating meat possible. And it makes hunting subversive within the context of globalization and the hegemony of corporate food production over individuals and families, and of corporate finance over corporate food production.

Clergy have been forbidden to hunt by a number of councils down through the centuries. But the reasons seem to have little to do with the killing of animals. In 1563 for example, the Council of Trent drew a distinction between "clamorous" and "quiet"[2] hunting. The former generally involved large and expensive packs of dogs, stables of horses, the privilege of land access and partying, and servants to see to all the foregoing, and so it was forbidden to the clergy; the latter involved none of these things and hence was allowed. Similar concerns, under the banner of secular class resentment, seem to have motivated the popular outcry against fox hunting in the UK some years ago. Fox hunting may be cruel, but we are mostly insulted that it is the preserve of the privileged few. At any rate, cruelty is a concept that is very quickly relativized in the context of the animal world. A bullet is a comparatively quick and painless end when one considers the destiny of animals left to their own devices in the wild.

But the Spanish philosopher (and hunter) José Ortega y Gasset once said that man does not hunt so that he may kill, rather he kills so that he may have hunted.[3] This distinction may be lost on the nonhunter. But hunting for me is as much, or more, about eating with integrity, and spending time with friends in the primary reality of creation. It is about the delight and deep satisfaction born of the necessity of becoming familiar with the ways animals behave, what they eat, and how they interact with the weather, the topography, and one another. My most satisfying duck hunt was one on which I never fired my gun. I sat in the cattails as dawn broke, talked to the ducks with my call, heard them talk back, and watched them circle overhead coming in to land among the decoys, apparently satisfied that I was one of them.

I once spent days driving and walking over land that I had been hunting for years, ostensibly looking for hogs, but finding none, realizing that I was in fact bidding farewell to hills and creeks that I loved, that had become a secret part of myself, and

2. Council of Trent, "Session 24," chap. 12.
3. Ortega y Gasset, *Meditations*, 105.

that I would see no more because my friends had decided to sell the ranch. I sat in my truck and wept.

Or there was the time, years ago, I went quail hunting with my cousin in south Georgia, riding home at the end of the hunt, the smell of pine trees and horses, saddle leather and gunpowder mixing in the air, the mule wagon creaking rhythmically along the ruts behind me, the woods green and golden and brown as the sun was setting. My uncle's recent death in a car crash, not far from the place we were hunting, weighed heavily that afternoon. But I was also rejoicing at the recent birth of the fifth generation of that land's stewards, my cousin's beautiful little girl. I was so contentedly intoxicated by the atmosphere that I almost fell out of the saddle, the two-man limit of quail in the wagon a mere punctuation mark at the end of the day's eloquence.

The French Dominican priest and World War II resistance fighter, Raymond Léopold Bruckberger, once wrote concerning America:

> Here, the land has not yet entered into communion with man, and man has not penetrated the mystery of the immense natural forces that shelter him. This land is terribly in need of blessing. The land is perhaps the promised bride of man, but she is not yet his. Most often she refuses to give herself or submits against her will. The land and man do not know each other in the flesh and in the spirit.[4]

God has entrusted to us the task of being faithful and wise stewards of the land, not just gazing longingly at her contours, but coaxing them firmly and gently into fruitfulness. We are meant to be custodians of the mystery of nitrogen, minerals, and water becoming stalks of millet and corn, husks of rice, sunflowers, or pine trees. Individual opportunities to realize this vocation are becoming increasingly rare and precious as they are offloaded onto the algorithms of autonomous machines, irrigation systems governed by photocells and barometers, GPS guided combine harvesters, and industrial feedlots run by clocks and computers.

4. Bruckberger, *One Sky*, 115–116.

But last weekend I rose hours before dawn, put on my boots, and drove out into the countryside. I took out my shotgun, shouldered a dozen decoys, and followed a familiar network of furrows through a soybean field to the edge of a pond. The wind was chilly out of the north, and the clouds were low as I set up and marked the minutes to legal shooting time. Before long I heard a familiar rush of wings from behind me as a flock of blue-winged teal dove low over the spread, circled around, and came back in. I missed more than I hit that morning, but that is beside the point. Back home, as I was dressing the birds, their blood and feathers warm and sticky and beautiful on my hands, I thanked God for the intricate mystery of it all, for the life that had been theirs and was now mine, for the food they were becoming, for land and friendship and water, and for the grace of divine nourishment at every level of the world's being.

14

EPILOGUE: IMPALA

For as long as I can remember, I have marinated and delighted in the natural world: hiking and camping during my teenage years as a Boy Scout, birding, amateur botany, and most of all, fishing and hunting. A thread running through all of it has been learning the names and the habits of the living things that share my world. This experience of the primary realties of nature has led, in what seems to me to be an inexorable way, to a delight in them and a corresponding desire to engage with them more intimately.

For most of my adult life, I have felt impelled to understand the ecology of the places I have lived, what flora and fauna lived there historically, when the structure of the biosphere was minimally affected by human input, what flora and fauna live there now, and how natural processes, species composition, and the like have changed because of increasing human interference. I have spent many days walking through the Trinity Forest in Dallas County, Texas, a riparian corridor along the Trinity River comprised of about ten thousand acres of virgin hardwood forest, one of the largest urban forests in the world. It is superficially untouched by human input, because much of it lies in a floodplain, unsuited to development. But changes forced upon the river—from being dammed and dredged, having its course altered to accommodate urban development, to pollution, runoff, and erosion—have compelled the forest, which takes its life from the river, to change also.

Meditating on the natural world has led me to deeper questions, more in the domain of philosophy than the natural sciences. What makes something "natural" or "unnatural"? We tend to think of "unnatural" things as somehow conspicuously marked by human input, yet this assumption leaves the activities of conservation and stewardship unaccounted for as categories of human input that result in the *restoration* of parts of nature that had been degraded by other kinds of human input. It also ignores the fact that, whatever more we might be, humans too are natural phenomena, and the instruments of ecological degradation themselves ultimately come from the earth—bulldozers, for example, are made largely of metal, and that metal was mined from the ground.

Common intuitions about what is natural and what is unnatural also leave unaccounted for the fact that manifestly natural processes, especially over long periods of time, can (and do) result in drastic alterations to the ecosphere far greater than even the most drastic human inputs—solar cycles and geologic processes that result in drastic climate change, the advance and withdrawal of glaciers, volcanic eruptions, and asteroid strikes (like the one that almost certainly caused the extinction of most life on earth at the end of the Cretaceous period). During the Cretaceous and Eocene, crocodiles and palm trees flourished in what is now northern Wyoming and southern Canada, before being eradicated by natural processes. It is impossible to think of such events and their outcomes as moral catastrophes.

Yet ecological degradation that is the result of human input is another matter. Precisely because it is marked by human action, and human action has a moral character, the ecological degradation of our time rightly provokes indignation and anger. We human agents might have acted in some other way, but instead we acted in *this* way. Our actions with respect to the natural world, like all of our actions, are deliberate, colored by reason and desire.

The question then becomes how we might form our desire in such a way that the pursuit of what we desire is less degrading, so that it is at least sustainable, to use a hackneyed term. And that, under a certain aspect, is the subject of this volume—the formation of desire. Most fundamentally, it is the progression from experiencing nature to delighting in it and desiring to know it that has led me to regard hunting as the highest form of engagement with the primary realties of nature.

Many look skeptically on the claim of hunters to love wildlife. On the surface, loving a thing would seem to be incompatible with trying to kill it, and I have often felt this tension, sometimes acutely, when I have miffed a shot, and an animal is wounded and not killed outright. But it is love for my quarry that underwrites my grief on such occasions, the feeling that my actions have failed to correspond to the dignity of the creature I was hunting, even though it be the result of carelessness or an honest mistake. Others too have noticed this apparent paradox:

> The hunter deeply respects and admires the creatures he hunts. This is the mysterious, ancient contradiction of the real hunter's character—that he can at once hunt the thing he loves. . . . Part of the hunter's deep attachment to wildlife may stem from the fact that he sees wild creatures at their best—when they are being hunted. It is then they are strongest, freest and sharpest.[1]

Yet all loves exist in a hierarchy and must be ordered aright, proportionate to one another and to their objects. I love mesquite wood for the flavor it conveys to meat in the smoking process, yet my love is not only compatible with the burning of the wood, but a function of it. I love the way the sun sets at Spanish Point, Bermuda, but my love for it is contingent on what precedes and follows it; I would not want my life to consist of one, long, continuous sunset at Spanish Point. My love for my wife is again different, higher, less contingent, subordinate only to my love for God. The love of the hunter for his quarry lies somewhere in the middle, higher and less contingent than his love for mesquite wood or sunsets, and lower than his love for his wife.

---

1. Madson and Kozicky, "The Hunting Ethic," 12.

The hunter's love is, to a significant extent, born of his familiarity with wild creatures, of his experience of them at their best, at their "strongest, freest, and sharpest."[2] Precisely such animals make the best trophies. Indeed what makes them "best" is their being situated at the top of the social hierarchies of their species, and they come to be there by being "best"—strongest, freest, sharpest. These individuals are the biggest, the oldest, the most fully developed. The ideal trophy animal sits precisely at the narrowest apogee of its development, at the instant before the aging process begins to make it more susceptible to disease, predation, or competition from its juniors.

One of my most prized trophies was an old impala, big bodied, thick horned, one horn broken off a third of the way up from fighting with some rival. I watched him, proud and alert in his harem, standing in the shade of a bush willow. I squeezed the trigger, saw him lunge, and found him dead about fifteen yards away in a dry stream bed. As I ran my hands over his bright fur, there was, as ever, a note of grief in my regard—grief that his career, his life, was ended. But my grief was colored by gratitude for what he had been and what he was spared, a fate arguably less compatible with his dignity—weakened by disease or a broken limb, excluded from his herd, starved, eaten alive by vultures or a leopard. And gratitude, too, for what he would become—my memory, my food. Every creature dies, and I had killed this one. But I had killed him quickly, at his strongest, freest, and sharpest, and I would incorporate him into my body and mind as food and memory.

Maximus the Confessor said that "what the pure intellect sees naturally through reverent knowledge it can also passively experience, becoming through its habit of virtue, the very thing it sees."[3] Yet to eat a thing is surely an even more intimate form of relational engagement than seeing. This intimacy is captured by the adage: "You are what you eat." It suggests the identity relation as constitutive of the relationship between the eater and the eaten. There can be no relation more intimate than that of identity,

2. Madson and Kozicky, "The Hunting Ethic," 12.
3. Maximus the Confessor, *Ambigua*, 205.

insofar as identity is the relation that a thing bears uniquely to itself. Even granting the poetic character of this adage, it nevertheless captures a deep truth about eating. The substance of what is eaten is transmuted by the processes of digestion and metabolism into the substance of the eater. The predator incorporates its prey into the most fundamental fabric of its material being. The predator quite literally *embodies* its prey.

For the Christian hunter, this dynamic is redolent of eucharist. Yet in the eucharist the symbolism is more multivalent, since what is consumed is the body of the "Lion of the tribe of Judah" (Revelation 5:5)—the apex predator *par excellence*. If you are indeed what you eat, we might infer that the Christian communicant himself becomes the "lion" he has consumed, a lion that has submitted himself to being consumed. "Out of the eater came something to eat, out of the strong came something sweet," as Samson put it in the riddle he posed to his Philistine in-laws (Judges 14:4). Christian communicants are thus in some sense "lionized," becoming predators who offer themselves as prey "for the life of the world" (John 6:51), precisely in virtue of their preying on the archetypal predator.

This spiritual subversion of the predator-prey dynamic has profound implications for the Christian hunter who ought to understand himself not only as a consumer, the utilizer of a resource, but as one whose life becomes so intertwined with what he utilizes and consumes that he is thereby fundamentally reoriented toward his prey; his life becomes, in a certain sense, *for* the life of the animals he hunts, for all that sustains them, for their and his habitat, for the world he shares with them. The hunter must be consumed, in the metaphorical sense, by what he consumes in the literal sense.

But the intimacy of hunting ripples out further into the subsidiary activities that constitute hunting as a unitary experience. It is necessary, for example, that the hunter understand at least the rudimentary habits of his quarry: what it eats; where it lives and feeds; the kinds of habitat it prefers; when and how it moves; how weather affects its behavior. In order to dress his quarry, to turn it into food, the hunter must understand something of its anatomy, organ and muscle groups, bone structure, and the like. And this intimacy likewise extends to the hunter's knowledge of himself, the limits of his skill, endurance, and strength.

It is this intimate experience of the primary realities of nature, of the layers of their interconnection, and of my own embeddedness within them, that I cherish most about hunting. It is what leads me to place hunting at the top of my hierarchy of experiences in nature.

Pseudo-Dionysius the Areopagite said that salvation is that, "which preserves things in their proper places without change, conflict, or collapse toward evil, that keeps them all in peaceful and untroubled obedience to their proper laws . . . this Salvation, benevolently operating for the preservation of the world, redeems everything in accordance with the capacity of things to be saved."[4] This is the form of conservation to which Christians, and all people of good will, are summoned in virtue of their common humanity. That is to say, it is not only for "conservationists" as such, let alone hunters, nor even merely for those who engage in a deliberate way with nature. It is an aspiration toward which duty calls each of us, a form of living in accord with what is true, what is real.

Properly therefore it ought to underwrite every experience of nature, to be lurking in the background of every apprehension of nature. As Ransom noted, it is impossible to love "a mere turnover, such as an assemblage of 'natural resources,' a pile of money, a volume of produce, a market, or a credit system,"[5] certainly not in the way a farmer may love his land, or indeed a hunter his quarry. In the final analysis *love* is the key ingredient, a participation in the benevolent regard of God on the sixth day of creation, seeing all that has been made and judging that it is, and that it should remain, "very good."

4. Pseudo-Dionysius, *Divine Names*, 896D–897A.
5. Ransom, "Reconstructed but Unregenerate," 20.

BIBLIOGRAPHY

Abbey, Edward. *A Voice Crying in the Wilderness (Vox Clamantis in Deserto): Notes From a Secret Journal.* New York: St. Martin's, 1989.

———. *Desert Solitaire.* New York: Touchstone, 1990.

Aquinas, Thomas. *Catena Aurea.* Translated by John Henry Newman. Eugene, OR: Wipf & Stock, 2005.

Aristotle. *On the Parts of Animals.* Translated by C.D.C. Reeve. Indianapolis: Hackett, 2019.

Auden, W. H. *Collected Poems.* New York: Vintage, 1991.

Augustine. *Confessions.* Translated by Henry Chadwick. Oxford: Oxford University Press, 2008.

———. *Confessiones.* https://faculty.georgetown.edu/jod/latinconf/latinconf.html

Babcock, Havilah. *My Health Is Better in November.* Columbia: University of South Carolina Press, 1985.

Bacon, Francis. *Valerius Terminus: Of the Interpretation of Nature.* Project Gutenberg, 2002 (originally published 1734). https://ebooks.adelaide.edu.au/b/bacon/francis/valerius/

Berry, Wendell. *What Are People For?* Berkeley: Counterpoint, 1990.

Bruckberger, Raymond Léopold. *One Sky to Share: The French and American Journals of Raymond Leopold Bruckberger.* Translated by Dorothy Carr Howell. New York: P. J. Kennedy & Sons, 1952.

Buckingham, Nash. *The Best of Nash Buckingham.* New York: Winchester, 1973.

Council of Trent. Session 24. "Chapter 12, 1563." In *Hanover Historical Texts Project*, edited and translated by Waterworth, 193–32. London: Dolman, 1848. https://history.hanover.edu/texts/trent/ct24.html

Dearmer, Percy, et al., eds. *The English Hymnal.* London: Oxford University Press, 1933.

De Crevecoeur. *Letters from an American Farmer.* Edited by Albert E. Stone. Harmondsworth: Penguin, 1981.

Deneen, Patrick. *Why Liberalism Failed.* New Haven: Yale University Press, 2018.

Derrida, Jacques. *On the Name*. Translated by David Wood. Stanford: Stanford University Press, 1995.

Descartes, René. *Discourse on Method*. Translated by Veitch. Project Gutenberg, 2008. http://www.gutenberg.org/files/59/59-h/59-h.htm

Eliot, T. S. *Collected Poems*. New York: Harcourt Brace, 1988.

Episcopal Church. *The Book of Common Prayer*. New York: Oxford University Press, 1979.

Francis. *Laudato Si'*. San Francisco: Ignatius, 2015.

"From Benjamin Franklin to Peter Collinson, 9 May 1753," *Founders Online*, National Archives, https://founders.archives.gov/documents/Franklin/01-04-02-0173. [Original source: The Papers of Benjamin Franklin, vol. 4, July 1, 1750, through June 30, 1753, ed. Leonard W. Labaree. New Haven: Yale University Press, 1961, pp. 477–486.]

Gavitt, Loren, ed. *Saint Augustine's Prayer Book: A Book of Devotion for Members of the Episcopal Church*. West Park: Holy Cross, 1999.

Harrington, Michael. "Creation and Natural Contemplation in Maximus the Confessor's *Ambiguum* 10:19." In *Divine Creation in Ancient, Medieval, and Early Modern Thought: Essays Presented to the Rev'd Dr Robert D. Crouse*, edited by Michael Treschow et al., 191–212. Leiden: Koninklijke Brill, 2007.

Hauerwas, Stanley. "The End of American Protestantism." https://www.abc.net.au/religion/the-end-of-american-protestantism/10099770.

Havel, Václav. "Politics and Conscience." In *Open Letters: Selected Writings 1965–1990*, translated by Erazim Kohak et al., 249–71. New York: Vintage, 1992.

Herbert, George. *The Temple*. London: T. Fisher Unwin, 1883.

Hopkins, Gerard Manley. *Poems and Prose*. London: Penguin, 1985.

Horace. *Opera*, edited by H. W. Garrod. Oxford: Clarendon, 1901.

Hugh of St. Victor. *The Didascalicon*. Translated by Jerome Taylor. London: Aeterna, 2020.

Jeffers, Robinson. *The Wild God of the World*. Stanford: Stanford University Press, 2003.

John of Damascus. *An Exact Exposition of the Orthodox Faith*. Translated by S.D.F. Salmond. A Select Library of Nicene and Post-Nicene Fathers of the Christian Church, edited by Schaff, et al., series 2, vol. 9. Grand Rapids: Eerdmans, 1996.

Madson, John, and Ed Kizicky. "The Hunting Ethic." *Rod and Gun* 66.3 (1964).

Kierkegaard, Søren. *Concluding Unscientific Postscripts to Philosophical Fragments*. Translated by Howard V. Hong and Edna H. Hong. Princeton: Princeton University Press, 1992.

Lewis, C. S. *That Hideous Strength*. New York: Scribner, 2003.

Matthiessen, Peter. *The Tree Where Man was Born*. New York: Penguin, 1995.

Maximus the Confessor. *On Difficulties in the Church Fathers: The Ambigua*, Vol. 1. Translated by Nicholas Costas. Cambridge: Harvard University Press, 2014.

Newman, John Henry. *Parochial and Plain Sermons*. San Francisco: Ignatius, 1997.

Ortega y Gasset, José. *Meditations on Hunting*. Belgrade: Wilderness Adventures, 1995.

Palmer, G. E. H., et al., eds. *The Philokalia*, Vol. 2. London: Faber and Faber, 1990.

Parmenides. "The Real." In *The Portable Greek Reader*, edited by W. H. Auden, translated by John Burnet, 77–80. New York: Penguin, 1977.

Pieper, Josef. *Leisure: The Basis of Culture*. San Francisco: Ignatius, 2009.

Pollan, Michael. *How to Change Your Mind: What the New Science of Psychedelics Teaches Us About Consciousness, Dying, Addiction, Depression, and Transcendence*. New York: Penguin, 1999.

Pseudo-Dionysius. *Divine Names*. In *The Complete Works*. Translated by Colm Luibheid. New York: Paulist, 1987.

Radner, Ephraim. *Chasing the Shadow—The World and Its Times*. Eugene, OR: Cascade, 2018.

———. "No Safe Place Except Hope: The Anthropocene Epoch." https://livingchurch.org/covenant/2016/07/28/no-safe-place-except-hope-the-anthropocene-epoch/

———. *The World in the Shadow of God*. Eugene, OR: Cascade. 2010.

Ransom, John Crowe. "Reconstructed but Unregenerate." In *I'll Take My Stand: The South and the Agrarian Tradition*, 1–27. Baton Rouge: Louisiana State University Press, 1977.

Ratzinger, Joseph. *In the Beginning: A Catholic Understanding of the Story of Creation and the Fall*. Translated by Boniface Ramsey, O.P. Grand Rapids: Eerdmans, 1995.

———. *Jesus of Nazareth: From the Baptism in the Jordan to the Transfiguration*. Translated by Adrian J. Walker. New York: Doubleday, 2015.

Scruton, Roger. *How to Think Seriously About the Planet: The Case for an Environmental Conservatism*. Oxford: Oxford University Press, 2015.

Shellenberger, Michael. "The Bigotry of Environmental Pessimism." https://quillette.com/2019/08/15/the-bigotry-of-environmental-pessimism.

Solomon, Christopher. "When Birds Squawk, Other Species Seem to Listen." https://www.nytimes.com/2015/05/19/science/decoding-the-cacophony-of-birds-warning-calls.html?_r=0

Taylor, Charles. *A Secular Age*. Cambridge: Belknap, 2007.

Teresa of Avila. *The Way of Perfection*. Vol. 2 of *The Complete Works*. Translated by E. Allison Peers. London: Continuum, 2002.

Tolstoy, Leo. "Letter to Dr. Eugen Heinrich Schmitt." In *Essays, Letters, Miscellanies*, translated by Aylmer Maude, 2:42–45. New York: Charles Scribner's Sons, 1913.

Warren, Robert Penn. "Foreign Shore, Old Woman, Slaughter of Octopus." In *Selected Poems*, 220–221. New York: Random House, 1976.

Weeks, Jerome. "For Earth Day: Texas Author John Graves." https://artandseek.org/2011/04/22/for-earth-day-texas-author-john-graves/

Weingarten, Debbie. "Why Are America's Farmers Killing Themselves?" https://www.theguardian.com/us-news/2017/dec/06/why-are-americas-farmers-killing-themselves-in-record-numbers.

Wittgenstein, Ludwig. *Culture and Value*. Translated by Peter Winch. Chicago: University of Chicago Press, 1984.

———. *Philosophical Investigations*. Translated by G. E. M. Anscombe. Englewood Cliffs: Prentice-Hall, 1958.

———. *Tractatus Logico-Philosophicus*. Translated by B. F. McGuiness, et al. New York: Routledge, 1961.